An Introduction to ULSTER ARCHITECTURE

Hugh Dixon

First published by the
Ulster Architectural Heritage Society, 1975

This edition published 2008 by the
Ulster Architectural Heritage Society
66 Donegall Pass, Belfast

Text copyright © H. Dixon 2008
Photographs copyright © Various: Anthony Merrick;
The Environment & Heritage Service; The National Trust;
Tony Corey; Ulster Architectural Heritage Society.

All rights reserved. No part of this publication may
Be reproduced, stored in a retrieval system or
Transmitted in any form or by any means, electronic,
Mechanical, photocopying, scanning, recording or
Otherwise, without the prior written permission of the
Copyright owners and publisher of this book.

British Library Cataloguing in Publication Data.
A catalogue record of this book is available from the British Library

Designed by April Sky Design, Newtownards
Printed by GPS Colour Graphics Ltd

ISBN: 978-0-900457-69-2 (hardback)

Large Format Landmark Series, No. 1
General Editor: Terence Reeves-Smyth

Front Cover:
St. Malachi's (C of I) Church, Hillsborough.
Photograph A.C.W. Merrick.
Back Cover:
Oval lantern, Upper Hall, Bellamont, Co. Cavan.
Photograph A.C.W. Merrick.
Title Page:
Chimney pots, Brownlow House, Lurgan,
Co. Armagh.
Photograph T. Corry (EHS)

Financial contribution towards publishing this book were
made by the Environment and Heritage Service;
Ulster Garden Villages; Marc Fitch Fund; Esme Mitchell Trust;
Edward and Primrose Wilson.

Contents

Introduction
9

Early Ulster
19

Plantation And Renaissance
49

The Eighteenth Century
83

The Nineteenth Century
127

The Twentieth Century
177

Bibliography
211

Index
217

Acknowledgements
224

Dedicated with gratitude
to the memory of

Professor Estyn Evans
Founding President of the Ulster Architectural Heritage Society
and
Sir Charles Brett
Founding Chairman and second President
Whose pens matched the strength of bulldozers

and

to those who care about
Ulster's architectural heritage

Preface

An Introduction to Ulster Architecture was first published in 1975 as a contribution to European Architectural Heritage Year. It was never one person's book. It relied on the research of specialists and on their kindness in smoothing the roughest parts of my understanding. I realise now how much I owe to the willingness of friends and colleagues, many alas no longer with us, to share their structural enthusiasms.

I wish to express my thanks to all, and particularly to Frances Bailey, Mike Baillie, Brian Boyd, Ronnie Buchanan, Bruce Campbell, Ian Campbell, Roger Carr-Whitworth, J A K Deane, Caroline Dickson, Dorinda Dunleath, David Evans, Clare Foley, Alan Gailey, Anne Given, John Gray, Alan Harper, Colin Hatrick, Desmond Hodges, Jack Johnston, Leslie Kennett, Paul Larmour, Anne Loane, Rolf Loeber, Chris Lynn, Peter McGuckin, Robert McKinstry, Tom McNeill, Edward McParland, Ian McQuiston, Anthony Malcolmson, Annesley Malley, Harold Meek, Marion Meek, Charles Munro, Rory O'Donnell, Richard Oram, Harry Patton, Marcus Patton, Peter Rankin, Ann Martha and Alistair Rowan, Nick Sheaff, Dawson Stelfox, Joe Tracey, Brian Walker, Richard Warner, Roger Weatherup, Brian Williams, Peter Woodman.

Illustrations are vital to this book, and I am most grateful to all who have helped to assemble them: Tony Merrick for going to the far reaches of Ulster in all weathers to take the superb photographs which form so much of the book; to the Environment and Heritage Service: particularly Gail Pollock, as ever, and Tony Corry for help with the photography; Gareth Edwards for scanning and adjusting the photographs; and Mark Mulholland and Eoin Lennon for assistance with imaging. To Sharon Corcoran for indexing the present edition. The National Trust in Northern Ireland, particularly Christine Rogers, Maurica Lavery and Malachy Conway, for helping to supply photographs. And not least owners who have permitted access to their properties for photography

Particular gratitude is expressed to those whose financial support made publication possible: the Environment and Heritage Service; Ulster Garden Villages; Marc Fitch Fund; Esme Mitchell Trust; and Edward and Primrose Wilson.

My final thanks are to those whose encouragement led to this new edition. Peter Marlow, as Chairman of the UAHS, first insisted on it; and Fiona agreed. Karen and Colin Latimer allowed a remote author to become "the lodger" in kindest of circumstances; and Karen's advice and editorial help have been vital. Terence Reeves-Smyth, Editor of this series, has been a model of assistance and patience; assembling illustrations, and tactfully sharing the updating of the text. This book is as much theirs as mine.

Lastly, my thanks and love to Jill Kennett who compiled the index to the original book, and who for the last thirty years has brought the same care and resolution to her roles of wife and mother.

HD
Oakwood, Hexham, Northumberland
February, 2008

Introduction

INTRODUCTION

Previous page: *Mount Panther, Co. Down. Entrance Doorway (c1770)*

Ulster's architectural heritage has, until quite recently, been too little appreciated. This book is designed as an introduction for the general reader: an attempt to present Ulster's building history in manageable form, covering in the broadest terms its development from the prehistoric period to the present day. To the specialist it offers only a broader horizon: some aspects have been studied for many years with patience and skill; but many others have remained almost unexamined. In consequence, anyone interested in the architecture of the province as a whole has, hitherto, been obliged to turn to a bewildering array of surveys, local histories, guides and gazetteers, antiquarian journals, architectural periodicals, directories, and even manuscripts - each dealing with some part, but only part, of the subject. The effort involved will have outweighed the curiosity of many people with only a casual or passing interest in the subject.

An introduction such as this must be, of necessity, highly selective; the choice of buildings illustrated and described has been governed by two principles. Firstly, a number of buildings have been included both because they are themselves important, and because they are already well known to Ulster people (sometimes for quite un-architectural reasons). It is hoped that these familiar stepping-stones will assist the reader in identifying the characteristics of successive styles, and relating them to a general development. Secondly, attention has been concentrated on those aspects of building which are peculiar to Ulster. Comparison with other places has sometimes led to the mistaken conclusion that Ulster has few architectural riches: while such comparisons may be instructive, they can also be prejudicial. No-one seeks Roman remains in America, but one might well explore the influence of Roman architecture on American buildings. Ulster, like America, has been subject to successive external influences, though over a much longer period. Like America, too, the province has absorbed these influences, developed its own building character, and produced its own architects. Yet Ulster is a small place, neither sufficiently close to be totally absorbed in the traditions of the neighbouring countries and provinces, nor sufficiently remote to offer effective resistance to all external influences. The result is that, while the buildings of Ulster often directly reflect stylistic changes in the rest of Ireland, in Britain and abroad, they do so with certain distinct and consistent characteristics which belong to the province alone. These derive from Ulster's own peculiar blend of geography, geology and history.

The choice of geographical limits to this study represents a compromise between the preferences of specialists in different periods. The legislative boundary between north and south is, in terms of the period covered by this book, very recent; the area of the ancient nine-county province of Ulster has many advantages. The pre-historian would probably favour a boundary further south; the medievalist might prefer to divide those eastern areas of Ireland which came under Norman influence from those western areas which remained wholly Irish; the student of modern architecture might claim that, since partition, official architecture in the six counties of Northern Ireland has had an influence which has not affected Monaghan, Cavan or Donegal.

INTRODUCTION

Above: *Waringstown House, Co. Down. Side View (1667)*

But at any rate for the period between, say, 1600 and 1921, the architecture of the nine northern counties, distinguished as they are from the rest of Ireland by variations in topography and climate, may be seen as sharing a distinctive flavour and character.

At least until the 19th Century, the character of Ulster's building was governed by the geological limitations of the province. With a few outstanding exceptions (sandstone from Cultra and Scrabo, Co. Down; limestone from Navan, Co. Armagh and Carrickreagh, Co. Fermanagh) local rocks are either too soft for durable building, or too hard to allow refined carving. This deficiency was to some extent offset by the establishment of brickworks in the 17th and 18th Centuries. The best bricks were made at Muff and Dunnalong, Limavady, Ballycastle, Ballymena, Lurgan and Coalisland. The bricks of Belfast proved particularly important, supplying not only the needs of the neighbourhood but also Downpatrick, Newry, and many other towns along the eastern coast.

In the 19th Century the difficulty of obtaining good building stone was, to a great extent, alleviated by the increasing industrial wealth of the province: quarries which had previously proved too expensive to work were reopened, and at

INTRODUCTION

Above: *Grey Abbey, Co. Down. West end of Cistercian Abbey church*

the same time large quantities of good carving stone were imported from England (Portland and Chester) and Scotland (Dumfries red and Scotch yellow sandstones especially from Giffnock near Glasgow, and granite from Aberdeen). Changes of style also assisted the popularity of local materials. Rough and mixed textures and brick pattern-work came to be admired. Marble, previously used almost exclusively for chimneypieces, now became popular for a wide range of decorative work. Ulster could supply a range of colours: white from west Donegal: light and blueish grey from north Donegal: cream from Chevy near Dungannon: light brown and dark red, strongly marked with fossils, from Co. Armagh.

Just as Ulster's geology influenced the design of its buildings, so its history has had a marked effect both on their character and their rate of survival. Repeated incursions brought strong foreign strains into the local building style. Repeated destruction and internal strife resulted in widespread damage, while rebuilding produced some curiously mixed styles. Attention has been directed in this study to the ways in which such varied origins and ragged development affected the external appearance of Ulster architecture. Waringstown House in County Down, begun in 1667, provides a fine demonstration of the merging of different traditions. The impressive symmetrical front, though simple in conception, has both the assurance of the Classical tradition and the self-conscious character of designed architecture. The second floor, itself a very unusual feature for a house of this date, seems to have been contrived from an attic storey and given regular

INTRODUCTION

Above: *New Forge House, Magheralin, Co. Down (c1770)*

windows. The lower wings add importance to the central block but they have, too, a slightly defensive character. The front door asserts its importance by crowding the windows which flank it and by pushing the point of its triangular pediment between the sills of the windows above. By contrast with all this centralised regimentation the side elevations have an agreeable jumble of Dutch and Scottish gables, a variety of windows and doors placed for convenience rather than style, and a devil-may-care arrangement of clustered Tudor Revival chimneys. Here it is the natural growth of local, or vernacular, architecture which predominates; for, despite the whimsies of style, and though the original thatching has been replaced with Welsh slates, the rendered walls of rubble and earth, bound with lime mortar, are perhaps the most typical feature of Ulster's native building tradition.

The mixed character of the province's buildings over the last three hundred years directly reflects the varied origins of those who designed them. In the 17th Century, much building design was done by people who had been born in

INTRODUCTION

Above: *Rosemount House, Grey Abbey, Co. Down. Garden Front (1762 & c1785)*

England, Wales or Scotland or even from further afield on the continent. They were often military or civil engineers or gentlemen- architects with a fancy for drawing; like the Normans before them, they brought their own architectural traditions. Ulster patrons in the 18th Century relied for the design of all but the simplest buildings on architects from outside the province, mainly from Dublin, Bristol, London, Cork, or Edinburgh. By the early 19th Century the Dublin influence was dominant; it was Dublin offices which generated designs for the great national architectural campaigns – churches of the Board of First Fruits and the Ecclesiastical Commissioners, county court houses, gaols and infirmaries, workhouses, and, later, coastguard stations, and many railway stations and banks. The case of the workhouses was perhaps the most dramatic example of external influence. Although the architect to the Poor Law Commissioners, George Wilkinson, came from Oxfordshire (where he had designed a least three workhouses) he operated from Dublin. Between 1839 and 1845 he supervised the building of over a hundred and thirty workhouses in all parts of Ireland, including 43 in Ulster. Decently built, if Spartan in finish, they brought about an awareness (though hardly a love) of a simple Tudor style which though common in England was rare in Ireland. Perhaps even more influential was Wilkinson's book *The Practical Geology and Ancient Architecture of Ireland*, published in 1845, which, as well as showing an appreciation of Irish architecture, identified good building stone all over Ireland and even recorded the cost of supply from the quarries.

It was Dublin, too, which provided the impetus for the establishment of a local architectural profession, first at Newry and Belfast, later at Derry and elsewhere. The appointment from the 1830s of County Surveyors with responsibility for public works (and often a capacity to take on private ones as well) was another important step in this development. With the advantages of growing industrial wealth, an abundance of appropriate materials, and local designers of outstanding ability, Ulster's architecture developed an increasing independence as the 19th Century progressed. Nevertheless, despite changing styles, changing patrons, and changing architects, the basic characteristics of Ulster architecture remained unaltered until the 20th Century. It was modestly scaled, undemonstrative, somewhat solid in aspect, usually restrained (sometimes even austere) in its use of external decoration; yet it was as varied as the people who created it, and as the landscape which it occupied. New Forge House, at Magheralin, built for Mr Waddell who operated a mill and bleach works, has a typically

Left: *Bellamont, Cootehill, Co. Cavan (Lovett Pearce c1730)*

INTRODUCTION

sober front with neatly arranged elements and decoration confined to a modest Classical doorway based on a pattern book design published about 1785. This reserve and lack of ostentation runs as a continuous theme through the progress of Ulster building. It is even there in parallel with the most hectic developments of the Victorian revivals; for every building with polychrome brick work or busy sculptural façades there must be at least a handful with smooth rendered elevations barely disturbed by thin pilasters or a few Italianate features.

In contrast, too many buildings erected in Ulster during the first three-quarters of the 20th Century lacked these specifically Ulster characteristics. In pursuit of international fashions some architects, overlooking traditional local qualities, produced buildings that were at best derivative and uninteresting, at worst strident and visually obtrusive. A lack of public confidence in contemporary architecture resulted in an increased interest in conservation; this enthusiasm, in turn, encouraged more architects to concern themselves with the care and conversion of old buildings. The establishment of a school of architecture at the Queen's University of Belfast in 1965 increased in the profession a deeper appreciation of the local environment. There is more interest today in the historic buildings of Ulster than at any time in the past. Some architects are taking the trouble to seek again the essence of Ulster's building character, to recapture it in their designs, and to restore to the province an architecture which it can again call its own.

The study of Ulster buildings has changed beyond recognition since the first edition of this book appeared in 1975. Then a bibliography covered one, rather crowded, page. Now there are area listings, period and type studies, and even a few biographies. Not least, there are works - by Maurice Craig, James Stevens Curl, Edward Diestelkamp, Paul Larmour, T.E.McNeill, Edward McParland, Alistair Rowan, Jeanne Sheehy, Roger Stalley and many others - which recognise Ulster buildings in wider contexts. In addition with periodicals now devoted to Ulster buildings, there is broader discussion of buildings old and new.

Protection has advanced, too, with official 'Listings' on both sides of the border and, despite perennial concern about grant-aid levels, exemplary conservation work has been achieved – as can be seen in editions of *Taken for Granted* (HBC and RSUA). HEARTH, both as Housing Association and restoration revolving fund, has set an outstanding example, followed by others, for providing good old buildings with new leases of life. Some of the work of the Northern Ireland Housing Executive, in refurbishing old houses and providing new, bears comparison with public authority houses anywhere. Significantly, some good conservation work has been done without grant-aid. Old buildings are better recognised both for quality and market value. It is increasingly a paying proposition to keep old buildings well-repaired. The introduction of Conservation Areas has drawn attention to the importance of streetscapes and village character. Since 1993 successive *Buildings at Risk* catalogues (UAHS with EHS) have provided frank and sobering progress reports on the state of historic buildings in Northern Ireland. There is no room for complacency. There are still good old build-

INTRODUCTION

Above: *Mount Stewart, Co, Down. Entrance front (William Morrison, 1845-47)*

ings in the province in a poor state or in danger of being spoilt by inappropriate development. There are still delicate settings and streetscapes which need care. Yet, in what has been achieved over the last thirty years, there is also much cause for optimism.

Most heartening is the important part played by the local profession in both conservation and better modern design and planning. The Queen's University of Belfast has trained architects for over forty years and its graduates are now in the forefront of a lively local profession. The establishment of a new School of Architecture at the University of Ulster can only contribute further to this.

Insularity is avoided through part training or practice abroad but architects return to enrich the province. Most Ulster buildings of the last thirty years were designed by Ulster architects.

Since recognisable architectural activity started in Ulster four centuries ago, the situation has been almost entirely reversed. Then external influences were dominant and local traditions and character ignored. Now architectural practice has moved towards a satisfactory fusion of international awareness with local understanding. Such a balance is needed if the particular character of the Ulster architecture is to be carried safely forward.

EARLY ULSTER

EARLY ULSTER

Previous page: *Armagh Friary, Armagh City*
Below: *Ballykeel Portal Dolmen, Co. Armagh*

Prehistoric

Ulster emerges from pre-history with an extensive and varied architectural heritage already intact. The remains of huts were discovered in the early 1970s, at Mountsandel by the River Bann, Co. Antrim, dating from the Middle Stone Age (Mesolithic Period, commencing seventh Millennium B.C.). These were recognised as part of the earliest settlement yet found in Ireland and almost without parallel in Western Europe. The most distinctive structures showed as part-circles of post holes, which were angled inwards suggesting that the posts were drawn together at the top forming a framework probably covered in skins or turf. The evidence of large, central sunken hearths and other remains suggest a small hunting and gathering community living at the place at least for the winter months and returning for a succession of years.

More advanced economies, more settled communities and more organised resources of labour, through community activity or slavery, are suggested by the Megalithic or 'big stone' monuments first erected in the New Stone Age (Neolithic Period) beginning towards the end of the fourth millennium B.C. The size of these structures, such as portal dolmens and passage graves, testifies to the engineering skill of the early inhabitants; the court tombs peculiar to the north of Ireland demonstrate their originality and independence. Ballykeel Dolmen on the western slope of Slieve Gullion in south Armagh is typically impressive. Three uprights supporting a massive capstone measuring ten by eight feet once formed the principal chamber of a cairn ninety feet long. Much more of the cairn survives at a court tomb excavated 1979-82 at Creggandevesky, Co. Tyrone. The semi-circular open court was formed with dry-stone walling at least two metres high, skilfully revetted to resist the thrust of loose cairn material behind. A central entrance beneath a massive lintel gave access to a gallery of burial chambers roofed with stones set as 'corbels' each stone reaching out slightly further than those on which it rests.

Sometimes such monuments are found in association with extensive earthworks, as at the great ritual site, the Giant's Ring, south of Belfast. From the Bronze Age (c2000-300 BC) survive a number of stone circles such as the dramatic hilltop example at Beltany, near Raphoe, County Donegal.

Above: *Legananny Portal Dolmen in the snow, Co. Down*

Below: *Creggandevesky Court Cairn, Co. Tyrone*

Below: *Grianan of Aileach, Co. Donegal*

Iron Age And Early Christian

For the building historian the Iron Age (from c300 B.C.) melts imperceptibly into the Early Christian period. The great defensive linear earthworks at the Dorsey ('the gates') in County Armagh, with palisades which are directly contemporary with a ceremonial timber building at Navan Fort twenty miles to the north, suggests the development of wider tribal ambitions and influences, as well as the need for territorial defence. Two main types of defended enclosure may be distinguished. Hill forts are generally earlier in origin, very much rarer, larger and more elaborate. Designed essentially as strongholds they encircle hilltops, embracing an area often over a hundred yards in diameter. Of these perhaps the most spectacular is the fort which shares its name with the hill which it crowns, the Grianan of Aileach, County Donegal. This stronghold of the O'Neills of Ulster occupies the top of the hill over 800 feet above sea level. Three concentric earth ramparts, probably the earliest part of the defences, enclose a circular stone fort over seventy feet in diameter with internal terraces and galleries. Estimates for the time of construction are typically vague, ranging from early in the first millennium B.C. to the 6th Century A.D. Early histories record destructions by a rival king in 674, by the Vikings in 937, and, most decisively, in 1101 when in retaliation for the sacking of his own royal seat at Kincora, Murtogh O'Brien, Lord of Clare, specifically ordered the removal of stone. The fort owes its present appearance partly to the O'Neill kings and partly to the restorations of the energetic Dr. Walter Bernard of Derry who in the 1870s, with the advice of the antiquarian George Petrie, raised the walls from six to seventeen feet.

Ring forts are much smaller, averaging about thirty yards across, with enclosing banks of earth (raths) or stone (cashels). Relatively lightly defended (although thickly planted thorns may have made them more formidable) they seem essentially to have been protected farms, increasingly used during the first millennium A.D. for habitation or other purposes, such as nightfolds. Like the other defensive type, artificial islands (crannogs) which first occur somewhat earlier, they often continued in use during the medieval period, and even later.

Above: *Dromena Cashel, Co. Down*

Right: *Lisnagade, Co. Armagh. Raths from the air*

Of the many monasteries founded in Ulster during the 5th and 6th centuries some, such as Bangor and Armagh, achieved scholastic distinction and grew into large communities. Little is known of the original monastic buildings though they seem to have been of modest size and, initially at least, built largely of timber. This was clearly a matter of choice. Irish monks were well travelled and certainly knew of stone building traditions in Northumbria or on the continent. Sites could be well defended. Nendrum, on Island Mahee in Co. Down, which was occupied by the 8th Century, had three concentric enclosing walls. The arrangement of buildings within the monasteries, though usually according prominence to the church, was irregular. It seems that

Below: *Devenish, Co. Fermanagh*

Above: *Nendrum, Co. Down*

it was not until St. Malachy rebuilt Bangor as an Augustinian house early in the 12th Century that the formal planning of groups of buildings was introduced to Ulster.

The most typical distinctive feature to survive from Irish monasteries is the round tower. The existence of the earliest of these in the 9th Century has frequently, and probably correctly, been associated with the Viking raids; though it is clear from the 12th-Century Romanesque carving of some that this association can be too narrowly made. Remains of round towers are found from Nendrum and Drumbo, Co. Down, in the east to as far away as Tory Island far off the coast of County Donegal. They seem to have served variously as refuges, belfries, watch towers, and safes for the storage of valuable possessions. Among the most complete examples are those at Devenish Island, Co. Fermanagh, and at Antrim, The latter has walls four feet thick at the base and rises to a height of ninety-three feet. It is hardly surprising that this symbol of defiance should have become the principal hallmark of Celtic Revival architecture in the 19th Century (see p.66).

Below: *Kilmore, Co. Cavan.*
Round headed door.

ROMANESQUE

During the Early Christian period Ireland achieved eminence as a centre of designing activity especially of metal work, stone carving and manuscript illumination. But the buildings of the period are so fragmentary that they are barely distinguishable from their Romanesque successors. The earliest churches were built of wood and it seems clear that, as Irish builders started using stone, they kept some features which derived from accustomed timber building methods. These include walls projecting beyond the gable line (like a log cabin), sometimes called *antae* (from the Latin for forward). There are good examples at St. John's Point, Co. Down, and at the southern of the two Derry Churches on the Ards, Co. Down; the northern, later church has no *antae* perhaps suggesting that this feature soon became redundant. They may have supported timbers protecting the exposed ends of roof timbers or a shelter canopy. Similarly, projecting stones called corbels probably replaced projecting beams in performing supporting or securing functions.

Most of the churches that survive from before the 12th Century are severe stone rectangles with doorways tapering in towards the top, small windows, and only localised ornament. The two joined churches at Killevy, Co. Armagh, may have been built as much as two centuries apart but they share very similar features. More sophistication can be seen at Banagher, Co. Londonderry, where a chancel was added about 1150-1200 to the church built three or four generations earlier. Its impressive west doorway has an inner round arch but outside there is a massive lintel set over inclined sides all within a recessed square panel. There is a development in the building techniques and finish, too. The main church was built of large rubble but the chancel is of finely finished ashlar stone with mouldings to its window and chancel arch and at its outer eastern corners which show that the masons had become aware of the continental Romanesque style. The crucifixion scenes on the lintels at Maghera, Co. Derry and Raphoe, Co. Donegal, and the more elaborate 12th-Century doorway from Trinity Island, Lough Oughter, built into Kilmore Cathedral, Co. Cavan, show that the decorative carving of architectural features could often be as fine as that on the more celebrated high crosses. Of the apparently larger churches founded by St. Patrick and his followers, at Armagh and, traditionally, at Downpatrick, only fragments survive with a few tantalising descriptions, and it is not until the arrival of the Normans that substantial remains can be examined.

Below:
Banagher Church, Co. Londonderry

Below: *Duneigh Motte, Co. Down*

NORMAN

For Ulster the arrival of John de Courcy and his Norman adventurers in 1177 meant both a new organisation of society and a new architectural tradition. The basic pattern for the Norman castle was the combination of a strong point, high and defensible, with a lower protected courtyard. The majority were earthworks; a high mound, called a motte, was creating by carting up material dug from encircling ditches; the top was enclosed with a palisade and sometimes further defended by a wooden tower. The courtyard, or bailey, below was often slightly raised and also protected with palisades and ditches. Among the grander examples is at Dromore, Co.Down, set in a loop of the River Lagan. The motte, rising forty feet above the enclosing ditch, is set to command the landward approach, while the rectangular bailey is further protected by the river.

It is one of the oddities of Anglo-Norman castles in Ulster that the bailey is frequently missing. Sometimes, as with the massive motte overlooking the harbour at Donaghadee, the bailey may have been obscured by later development. Often, however, on less developed sites, no evidence for a bailey can be traced. This is the case at Dundonald, Co. Down, where the castle was captured by King John in 1210 and then destroyed by the Scots a century later. The Anglo-Norman presence in Ulster was very limited; away from the safe strongholds of the east coast motte-and-bailey settlements are increasingly rare. Some seem to have been built by Irish lords in imitation of their Norman neighbours though this influence does not continue west of the River Bann.

Above: *Clough Motte and Castle, Co. Down*

The motte-and-bailey castle at Clough, Co. Down, has added interest in the survival of stone buildings on top of the motte. A large hall survives only as buried footings but there is also a fragment of a later 13th-Century tower with an addition made when the building was re-occupied as a tower house perhaps about 1500. This move towards stone building was general. At first only the very powerful could afford the security, sophistication and convenience which stone castles provided. Gradually, as the Middle Ages progressed and when resources allowed, local lords strove to have their own towers.

Above: *Dundrum Castle, Co. Down*

As with earthworks the Normans constructed stone castles which combined a high place of strong defence with a lower protected areas. The strongpoint of their stone castles is the keep, which may be wholly or partially enclosed by the curtain wall defending the bailey or ward. Outer wards could also be enclosed by lower curtain walls, while gatehouses dominated the access at each stage. The main characteristic of Norman architecture is the massive wall. The style when applied to Europe as a whole is called Romanesque, being reminiscent of the ponderous strength of antique Roman building. The castle relied on the great thickness of its walls for defence. Externally the size of openings was kept to a minimum, but the windows were widely splayed inside to admit as much light as possible.

At Dundrum, Co. Down, John de Courcy started the great castle soon after his invasion of Ulster in 1177. He built the curtain wall around the upper part of the hill. The keep seems to date from after his downfall in 1203 when the castle was in royal hands or after it had been granted to Hugh de Lacy in 1227. The shape of the keep, a great cylinder, is of a type rare in England. Many of Ulster's Normans, however, originated in south Wales, where there is a massive cylindrical keep at Pembroke Castle. Dundrum seems to have an even closer cousin at Longtown, Monmouthshire (c1187). Both may have been built by members of the de Lacy family. When complete, by the end of the 13th Century, the defences at Dundrum included an improved gatehouse to the upper ward, and a lower ward with its own defended gate. The castle's final building phase came in the 17th Century when the Blundell family built a more comfortable house with wider windows, more hearths, and more convenient location in the lower ward. This shift from defensive priorities towards comfort and convenience was a pattern eventually followed all across the province with startling results as far apart as Dunluce and Donegal.

An early instance is to be found at Greencastle, Co. Down, where there was a large and strong hall built in the 13th Century, serving as a keep in the middle of a courtyard with corner towers. Much damaged by attack in the 14th Century and then neglected, the castle was radically changed by Sir Nicholas Bagnall after 1552. The hall was remodelled with wide regular windows and a large fireplace on the first floor, and various domestic buildings were added in the courtyard.

Below: *Greencastle, Co. Down*

Transitional

Much of the building undertaken by the Normans in the years following their first arrival in Ulster reflects the current development elsewhere in Europe from the round arches and dominating walls of the Romanesque style to the pointed arches and less oppressive Gothic manner. The nave at Grey Abbey, in County Down, dating from the early 13th Century (although much rebuilt) is an instance of this transitional style. The mass of the west wall is emphasized by the one window which squeezes from a wide round-topped splay on the inside of the wall to a narrow slit at the outside, as though it just manages to pierce the wall. By contrast the arches over the crossing in the foreground, which are of the same date, are pointed and divided into three stages. This gives them a much less hefty aspect. An even more striking example of this is

Below: *Greyabbey, Co. Down. The Refectory*

Above: *Inch Abbey, Co. Down*

the elaborate carving of the west door. A series of moulded arches spring from files of thin colonnettes set in the splay of the door, and, thus, what was one heavy feature now appears as a cluster of light elements.

At the contemporary Inch Abbey, County Down, the mass of the presbytery wall is so dispelled by three lancet windows with delicate colonnette mouldings that, for the first time, it is possible to refer to the style as Gothic.

Of the same age but built with much less elaboration by the poorer Third Order Franciscans is the Friary (founded 1264) now in the Palace grounds at Armagh City. The Friary was suppressed in 1542 and destroyed in the Elizabethan fighting in 1595. In the 18th Century the ruins became a useful quarry for new building in Armagh until Primate Robinson stopped this practice and incorporated what remained into his demesne. Only fragments of the 13th-Century church remain but these are enough to show that the great rubble walls had been relieved by wide windows and arcades with attached mouldings. This building, too, had moved without drama into the Gothic world.

Gothic

Gothic architecture is necessarily expensive; its fully developed form demands a unity of decorative features binding columns to walls and walls to window tracery and vaulting. Above all it seeks to break up the dominant strength of the Norman wall and by multiplying vertical elements to create a new, light, soaring architectural style. During the years which saw the great flowering of Gothic architecture in England and on the continent, Ulster lacked the booming economy which was necessary to foster the skills required to develop the style. With regard to materials the province was also at a disadvantage being without stone which could be easily carved and still remain durable.

But Ireland's social history has also been the cause of the apparently poor quality of its Gothic architecture; fragile and decorative by its nature, it has too often been the object of destroyers' attentions. Thus, while Ulster once had mature Gothic buildings such as the great cathedrals and religious houses at Armagh and Downpatrick, only the more solid and less decorative examples survive, and these only in fragments. For example, the early 14th-Century arcade of the Dominican Priory, at Newtownards, Co. Down, differs from the Transitional examples only in the decoration of its slightly pointed arches and the lightness of the thin columns which support them, The wall beyond, dating from the 17th Century, with its deeply splayed window embrasures, seems almost to return to the Norman tradition.

Below: *Newtownards Priory Arcade, Co. Down*

GOTHIC

Right: *Bonamargy window*

35

Natural Fortresses

That the advantages of building on natural fortresses were obvious to the Irish and Normans alike, may be judged by the number of ruins which dominate rocky headlands and natural crags throughout the province, and also by the prefix 'Dun' which often denotes the historic location of a fort especially when followed by a name (e.g. Dundonald).

Dunluce is among the most theatrical examples of the type, built on a rocky headland surrounded by sheer cliffs with the sea roaring through a great tunnel-cave below. Originating probably in early Norman times, it became during the late Middle Ages the northern stronghold of the powerful MacDonnell family. The castle was rebuilt and extended over the years and now forms an intriguing architectural puzzle, with early barrel towers and curtain walls, Scot-

Below: Dunluce Castle, Co. Antrim

NATURAL FORTRESSES

Above: *Kinbane Castle, Co. Antrim*

tish stepped gables and turrets, a gabled manor house, a curiously Italian-looking loggia, and a series of later buildings on the landward side of the narrow bridge. Other examples of natural fortresses are Dunseverick and Kinbane, both in Co. Antrim, and Dungannon, Co. Tyrone, for a long time a stronghold of the O'Neills.

Below: *Audley's Castle, Co. Down (c1480)*

TOWER HOUSES

Life in the parts of Ulster dominated by the Normans was probably never very peaceful. As the impact of the initial conquests subsided so the familiar pattern of border life increased. Raid was followed by counter raid; the strength of the Irish was realised and during the late Middle Ages the Anglo-Norman presence became a thin pale-beyond-the-pale along the Down and South Antrim coast. For those who could afford it the tower house became a necessity. In County Down a distinct type evolved which had its origins in the gatehouses of earlier, larger castles. Its plan was square with a small door set into the side wall of a recess and defended from above by an arched machicolation. Kilclief Castle (c1430) appears to be the earliest of the type but other good examples of the 15th Century are Audley's Castle, near Strangford, and Jordan's Castle at Ardglass. At Audley's, and perhaps elsewhere as well, the tower was attached to a walled yard which could be used to defend stock and stores in times of stress. The design was not always so elaborate; towers with plain square or 'L' shaped plans were also built and defended either by external machicolations or internal murder holes. The ground or first floor was commonly vaulted as a defence against fire and the upper chambers were reached either by spiral stairs in one corner of the tower, or by straight stairs in the thickness of the wall. At Narrow Water, built in 1568 for £361, the vaulted first floor has deep window embrasures and mural chambers in each of its corners, one for the stair and another for a latrine with external chute.

TOWER HOUSES

*Kilclief Castle,
Strangford,
Co. Down (c1435)*

Above: *Narrow Water Castle, Co. Down (1568)*

Ardglass Bay, Co. Down, with Jordan's Castle (c1530) on right; the ruins of Newark Castle to the left and Cowd Castle on the far left.

Kirkiston Castle, Ringboy, Co. Down (1622 with additions c1810)

Late Medieval Windows

Of church building activity in the late medieval period little is known and, indeed, probably little was carried out. From what survives it is only possible to say that the structures were simple, usually only a rectangular nave, and only the decoration of the windows gives an indication of date. Curiously precisely dated is the east window from St. Mary's Abbey Church, Devenish Island which was incorporated in the present Devenish Parish Church when it was rebuilt by Thomas Drew in 1890. An inscription on the island states clearly that the window was the work of Matthew O'Dubigan in 1449. The window is simple enough; separated by a single upright (mullion) two lights filled with stained glass rise to a decorated point with flame-shaped lights which derive ultimately from the French 'Flamboyant' style. Other similar examples at Culfeitrin, Co. Antrim and Balleeghan, Co. Donegal, have both flamboyant tracery and horizontal divisions (transoms) to the windows, suggesting a rather later date. It is the crossing of mullions and transoms (coupled with the gradually less pointed arch) which give the 'Perpendicular' style its name, though this is rare in Ulster until its extensive use in the Tudor Revival of the 19th Century (see Plate 58). Finally the pointed arch disappears altogether to be replaced by a square-headed window, like those at Antrim Parish Church (1596), with three trefoil headed lights and topped with a hood or label moulding.

Left: *Devenish Church, Monea, Co. Fermanagh*

LATE MEDIEVAL WINDOWS

Above: Culfeitrin, *Co. Antrim*

Above: *Antrim Parish Church (1596)*

EARLY ULSTER

MEDIEVAL SURVIVAL

Among the most remarkable medieval survivals in Ulster is St. Patrick's Cathedral at Armagh. Built on the site of a church which had existed since at least the 9th Century (which may itself have superseded St. Patrick's own 5th Century structure) the present building dates from the time of Primate Scannell who began building in 1268. Since that time the Cathedral has been repeatedly damaged either by war or neglect, and repeatedly patched and rebuilt. Apart from the 18th Century tower the external appearance derives from Primate Beresford's restoration of

Below: *St. Patrick's Church of Ireland Cathedral, Armagh*

MEDIEVAL SURVIVAL

1834, carried out to the somewhat heavy handed designs of L N. Cottingham, who rebuilt or refaced almost all the medieval building. The result is dull but stable. In detail however, especially inside, the cathedral has many excitements; good 17th and 18th Century monuments, a rakishly irregular plan with the nave aslant from the chancel, a medieval staircase leading up to the tower through the thickness of the south transept wall (its small windows can be seen in the photograph), and beneath the chancel a vaulted crypt with massive piers.

Below: *St Nicholas (C of I) Church, Carrickfergus, Co Antrim.*

EARLY ULSTER

MEDIEVAL TRADITION

The essence of medieval building tradition is the way it can develop through generations of designers and builders, through successive styles and fashions of living, and yet can retain in a single building venture a natural continuity. This is best demonstrated by the great cathedrals of the continent where centuries passed between foundation and completion. In Ulster the grandest example of such growth is Carrickfergus Castle where the need for successive changes has been met with remarkable resilience. The original late 12th Century castle with its gatehouse, curtain wall and keep was the only one to retain an Anglo-Norman garrison throughout the Middle Ages. In the face of increasingly efficient artillery the height of the gatehouse was lowered and at the same time brick-lined guns were set into its walls by Elizabethan engineers. The subsequent addition of Georgian barrack buildings, Edwardian gun emplacements and 20th Century museum has only emphasized the strength of this natural development.

Below: *Carrickfergus Castle, Co. Antrim*

MEDIEVAL TRADITION

Above: *Carrickfergus Castle, Co. Antrim*

Left: *Carrickfergus Castle*

Plantation And Renaissance

PLANTATION AND RENAISSANCE

Renaissance Carrickfergus

Previous Page: Image of Sir Arthur Chichester from the Chichester Monument, Carrickfergus

Carrickfergus was the base from which Elizabethan generals attempted to dominate Ulster through plantation. Their architecture reflects the need for defence and strategic communication before comfort. Thus Moyry Fort, County Armagh, built to preside over the southern approach to Ulster in 1601, is a business-like stone box liberally equipped with musket loops. It would fall happily into the category of square tower with an attached bawn, if its overwhelmingly defensive character did not completely outweigh domestic considerations. The tower's rounded corners are a rare feature in Ireland and are probably explained by the identity of the man who supervised the work, Levan De Rose, a Dutch engineer working for Lord Mountjoy, the Lord Deputy. The employment of continental designers, of which this is an early example, was to have important consequences in the introduction of Renaissance features and the development of Classical building in Ulster. Lord Mountjoy, for whom Moyry was erected, built an even more substantial fort at Charlemont (1602-1624) covering the crossing of the River Blackwater. This was a sophisticated up-to-date artillery fortification. Great earthworks with pointed bastions protected a central stone fort with flankers and a gatehouse and drawbridge. Inside all these defences it was possible eventually (the precise date is not clear) to build a comfortable governor's house of a kind then popular in England. Its whole character was governed by the Renaissance demand for balance and harmony with all the parts subject to the whole design. It had symmetrical façades, regular bays of windows, horizontal bands defining the storeys, and tall chimneys arranged in balancing groups. Its deliberate destruction as recently as 1920 is a shame because it was perhaps the most complete Renaissance building of its generation in the Ulster.

The grandest example of the type had an even safer haven within the new walls of Carrickfergus; this was Joymount, built about 1611 by Sir

Below: Joymount House and the town of Carrickfergus. Phillips view, 1680

Arthur Chichester. Wide windows spaced regularly across its three-storey façades gave a light interior unimaginable in thick-walled tower houses. Removed in the early 18th Century, the house may have had relatively little decoration or ornate stone carving but it was a clear echo of its magnificent English counterparts such as Longleat or Hardwick. In early 17th-Century Ulster it must have seemed startlingly light and convenient, and in the organization of its parts strikingly Classical and modern.

Left: *Charlemont, Co. Armagh. Illustration c1625*

PLANTATION AND RENAISSANCE

Below: *The Chichester Monument in St Nicholas's Church, Carrickfergus (c1622)*

PLANTATION CLASSICISM

The planters brought new architectural fashions as well as up-to-date methods of fortification. The Renaissance style in northern Europe begins with the modest quotation of Classical Roman features, columns supporting carved entablatures, semi-circular arches, and realistic sculpture. Frequently architecture follows the example set by monumental sculpture. The sophisticated monument set up by Sir Arthur Chichester in the transept which he added in 1614 to the medieval parish church of St. Nicholas at Carrickfergus was almost certainly not carved in Ireland. The exquisite detail of the columns, the enrichment of the arches betraying the influence of France and the Low Countries, and the confident poise of the sculpture, all point to this being the imported work of an English master mason. There are good parallels in Chichester's native west country. By contrast the monument in Lifford church to Sir Richard Hansard and his wife (a relative of Lord Mountjoy) is a more homely affair though of the same basic pattern, with two kneeling figures facing one another across a double lectern in an arched recess. Sir Richard survived his wife by only two days in 1619; the church, funded through his will, was built in 1622 and the monument would have been set up at this time.

Much more elaborate is the doorway in the north tower added to Newtownards Priory when it was restored as a residence after 1607 for Hugh Montgomery, one of the major Scottish settlers of County Down. Here the round-arched doorway has a variety of mouldings and enrichments.

PLANTATION CLASSICISM

Elaborately carved flanking pilasters support a Classical entablature with a decorated frieze and cornice. Above, set between biblical texts and obelisks, is a semi-circular pediment. In the centre of the frieze above the keystone of the arch is a monogram 'HLM' – apparently for Hugh Lord Montgomery, a striking example of Renaissance man putting himself at the centre of things. But the overall impression, typically Jacobean, is of a collection of pieces brought together for effect but lacking coherence and harmony. During the course of the century, with the help of pattern books, local masons mastered the proportions of the Classical orders and reproduced them with a good deal of lively invention. The Wolfenden Monument, Lambeg, (1693) combines a curving pediment with correctly tapering columns mounted rather oddly (but in the best Mannerist tradition of Michelangelo at the Laurentian Library, Florence, in 1524) on simple curved brackets.

Above: *Wolfenden Monument, Lambeg, Co. Down (1693)*

Above: *Monea Castle, Co. Fermanagh (1618-19)*

FORTIFIED HOUSES

The main initial concern of the planters was defence, and in the more remote parts of the province settlements had as their focus a fortified house. The planters naturally brought with them their own building traditions, so it is perhaps no surprise to find that the plantation houses have a strong English or Scottish flavour according to the origin of the builders. Castle Caulfield, Co. Tyrone (c1615) and the wing added by Sir Basil Brooke to Donegal Castle (c1625) both have features of contemporary or rather earlier English manor houses. Similarly many of the Fermanagh castles have a strong Scottish flavour with crowstepped gables, pepperpot turrets (bartizans), and turnpike staircases. A characteristic range of Scottish plans is found: T-shaped at Castle Balfour (1618) and Tully Castle, both in Fermanagh; square with corner towers at Roughan, Co. Tyrone (1618); star-shaped at Augher; and L-shaped at Derrywoone, Co. Tyrone. Perhaps the grandest of the castles was Monea, Co. Fermanagh, built by Malcolm Hamilton (1618-19). Two barrel towers flank the main entrance with their upper parts built out square on courses of corbels. From the sides of the towers musket loops were positioned to defend the walls. The effect is at once imposing and functional.

FORTIFIED HOUSES

It is clear, however, that there was Scottish influence before the plantation. Burt Castle, Innishowen, Co. Donegal, has a 'Z' plan with a central tower defended on two opposite corners by circular turrets. This is a very common type in Scotland but not in Ireland, yet Burt is described and drawn on a document dated 1599 when the castle was in the possession of Hugh O'Doherty.

Derrywoone Castle, near Baronscourt, County Tyrone, built by the Hamiltons about 1620, was originally of four storeys on an L-shaped plan with a large round tower at the point of the 'L'. In the inner angle of the 'L' a stairway supported at first-floor level on elaborate courses of corbels. Here, as at Monea and Castle Balfour, the character the carving is so Scottish that it is likely to have been the work of Scottish masons who arrived as part of the plantation.

Below: *Tully Castle, Co. Fermanagh (1612)*

PLANTATION AND RENAISSANCE

Above: Castle Caulfield, County Tyrone (c1615)

Right: Diagrammatic view of Castle Caulfield, County Tyrone

FORTIFIED HOUSES

Below: *Derrywoone Castle, Baronscourt, County Tyrone (c1620)*

PLANTATION BAWNS

Usually the plantation castle was accompanied by a bawn, a walled yard often defended at the corners by flanking turrets or 'flankers'. Sometimes the bawn exists alone with rather higher walls offering protection for less substantial but more comfortable houses within. Dalway's Bawn, Bellahill, north east of Carrickfergus, built by John Dallowaye in 1609, is one of the best surviving examples in the east of the province. At three of the four corners of a rectangular enclosure flankers jut out to give positions from which covering fire may be delivered. Nor were the flankers necessarily only defensive; when substantially built like this they provided normal living accommodation.

At Benburb, Co. Tyrone Sir Richard Wing-

Below: *Benburb, Co. Tyrone (c1611-14)*

PLANTATION BAWNS

Above: *Dalway's Bawn, Co. Antrim (1609)*

field chose to build his plantation stronghold on a site previously fortified by Shane O'Neill in the 1550s overlooking the Blackwater. The bawn was enclosed by a wall sixteen feet high pierced with musket loops. Two of the three surviving flankers are rectangular towers which, though placed for defence, have mullioned windows, and were intended for regular occupation. The third flanker is circular and has a turnpike stair originally giving access to the upper defences.

Plantation Settlement

Some of the largest bawns were built as headquarters for the plantations of the various London Companies in County Londonderry. Here the apparent lack of good local building stone and the proximity of ports at Coleraine and Derry, resulted in the import of timber-frame houses. These could be easily set up to provide a type of accommodation more familiar to the settlers but they were barely defensible and, of course, easily burnt. Not surprisingly, few survived the wars of the 17th Century. The more substantial houses, particularly those of the Company agents, usually within the bawn, were built of stone; their turrets and gabled fronts with high chimneys are a curious blend of English and Scottish traditions. These, too, have almost entirely disappeared though substantial sections of the bawns which originally defended them remain. Among the best surviving examples are those of the Fishmongers at Ballykelly, with four flankers each of a different shape, the Vintners at Bellaghy with a very large circular flanker, and of the Skinners at Dungiven and Brackfield. In many cases, in all the planted areas, the placing of castles and bawns had a lasting effect on the layout of the settlements which grew up about them. Streets were laid out from the bawn often in a grid pattern but with a main street leading to a focal market place. Here might be built a market or court house. The church was usually placed near the bawn, forming a manorial group. The other important building for the community was the mill which had to be placed where it could be powered usually by water. Not least important was the influence of communications. Traditional routes on good ground, river crossings and natural harbours all played a part in the shaping of Ulster's towns.

Right: *Fishmonger's house and bawn, Ballykelly, Co. Londonderry. Thomas Raven c1622. Phillips Mss.*

PLANTATION SETTLEMENT

Below: *Mercer's house, bawn and village, Moyvanagher, Co. Londonderry. Thomas Raven c1622. Phillips Mss.*

Below: *Model of a plantation village, Moneymore, Co. Londonderry*

PLANTATION AND RENAISSANCE

PLANTATION CITY DEFENCE

Below: *Map of Londonderry City, c1620, showing walls. Thomas Raven,. Phillips Mss.*

Singular among the settlements of the plantation both for its scale and the elaboration of its defences was the City of Londonderry. Built between 1609 and 1629 on the site of an ancient ecclesiastical centre, it occupied a crucial position at the mouth of the River Foyle. The present walls were begun in 1614, completed in 1618 and continually rebuilt and strengthened to meet the challenge of three major sieges during the course of the century. The walls were defended at

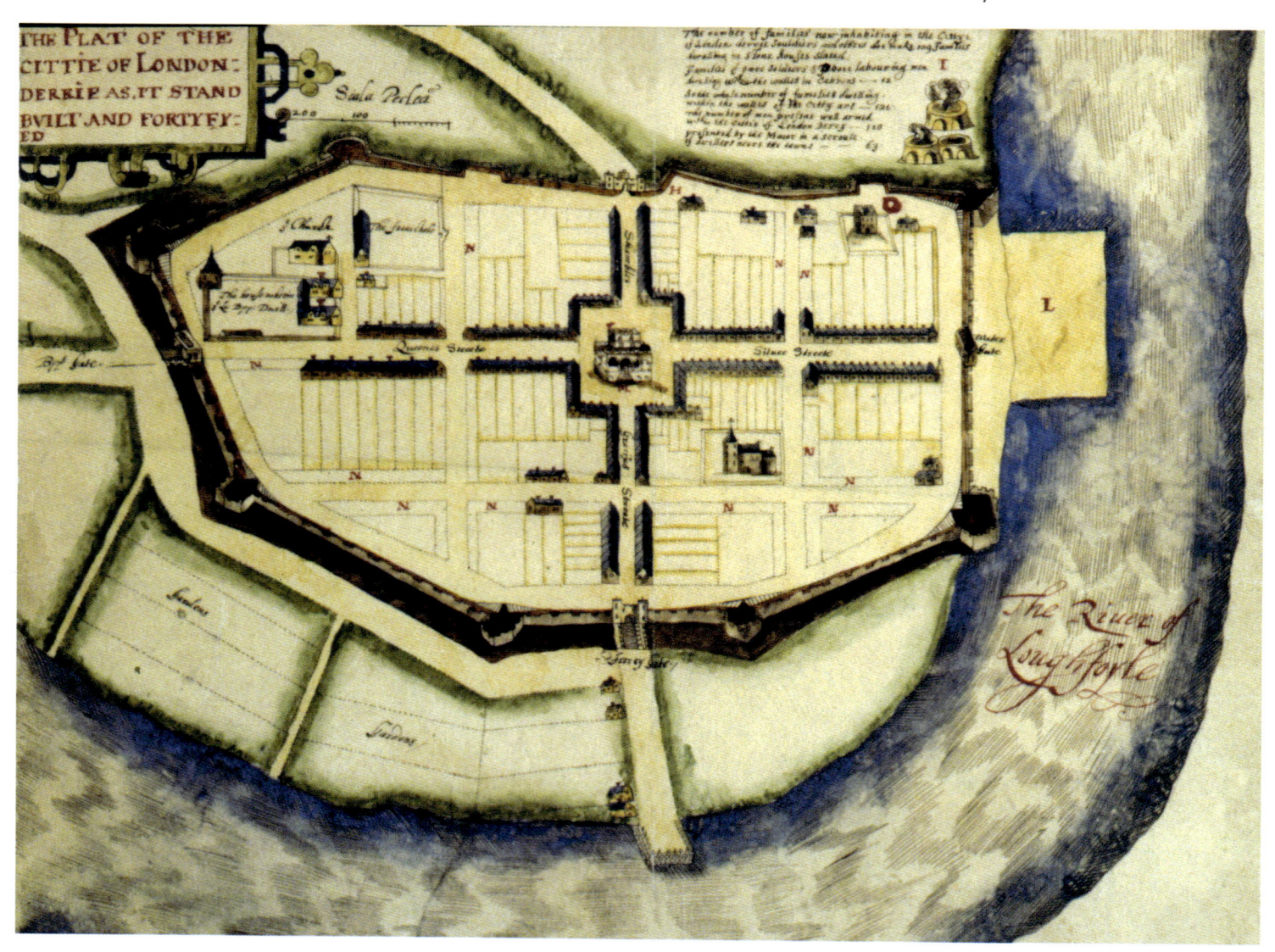

PLANTATION CITY DEFENCE

intervals by spear-shaped bastions wide enough to hold cannon. From gatehouses at the cardinal points of this strong perimeter four streets converged to meet in a central diamond. Other streets running parallel to these complete a regular grid. This formal treatment probably owes its origin as much to the planned towns of Edward I in Wales as to antique Roman examples. Nevertheless it demonstrates the Renaissance interest in organization which plays such a marked part in the layout of many plantation towns and villages. The style of buildings within the walls reflects the meeting of the medieval and Classical traditions; St. Columb's Cathedral (1628-33) was built in a late Gothic manner, while Phillips's fortified market house (1622) and Neville's Town Hall (1692) both designed to occupy the Diamond had Classical doorways and arcades. Outside the city a further fort was built to guard the narrows at Culmore; its gun-mounted bastions were a small version of the city's own defences.

Below: *Culmore Fort, Co. Londonderry*

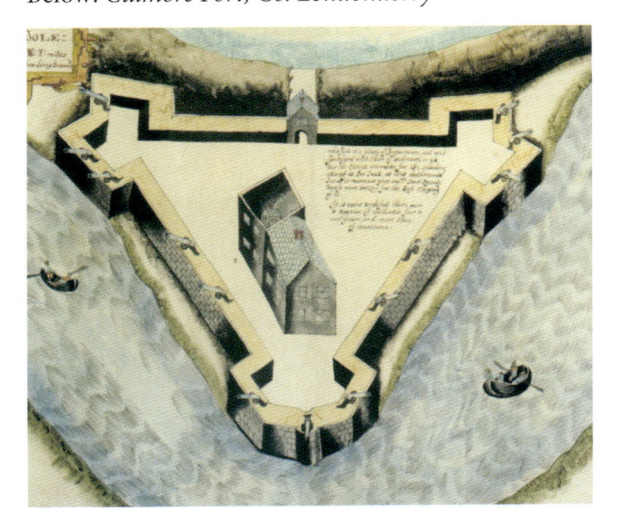

Below: *Londonderry City Walls*

Scottish High Houses

In several cases and more especially on the eastern side of the province Scots simply arrived and built Scottish houses. Ballygally Castle, built in 1625 by James Shaw of Greenock, has so much in common with other houses in Renfrewshire that it might as well have been built at Greenock on the Clyde. A simple rectangular tower rises to a steeply-pitched roof and a characteristically theatrical skyline of high chimneys, cone-topped bartizans projecting from the upper corners on corbels, and elaborately gabled dormer windows. It was the excitement of this kind of composition

Below: *Ballygally Castle, County Antrim (1625)*

which so appealed to both patrons and architects in the 19th Century and resulted in the extensive use, especially by those of Scottish descent, of revived Baronial style. The only feature which might mark Ballygally as an Ulster castle is the presence of the bawn with corner flankers much of which survives as a garden wall. Ballygally Castle, now an hotel, is one of the very few 17th-Century houses which remain in active use in Ulster.

Similarly placed near the shore, and just as Scottish, is the Old Custom House at Bangor, County Down, which was built in 1637 by Lord Clanneboye, a Hamilton from south west Scotland. Like Ballygally it is essentially a tall, gabled house though in this case it is defended by a full-height flanker tower on its most seaward corner. This very Scottish feature could have been used to provide flanking fire in any attack on the building but probably served more as a vantage from which to observe the passage of ships. Other baronial features include plain roll-mouldings around the window dressings, crow-stepped gables, and a stair corbelled out in the angle between the tower and the gable of the house. The rubble walls would probably have been covered originally, in the Scottish way, with lime rendering or harling as those at Ballygally still are.

Right: *Bangor Old Customs House, Co. Down (1637)*

PLANTATION AND RENAISSANCE

Plantation Churches

The shift in building fashion, from medieval Gothic to Italian Renaissance Classical, reached gradually to the northern fringes of Europe. It is best seen in Ulster not so much in the castles and bawns which had to be severely functional, as in the modestly scaled churches which the planters erected. Occasionally the shift can be seen in a single building. The east window of the small church built by Sir John Dunbar at Derrygonnelly, Co. Fermanagh, in 1623, has late Gothic windows with pointed ogee arches; but the round arch of the west door has facet-cut stones of a distinctly Italian character. Typifying the spread of Renaissance features, similar decoration is to be found elsewhere in northern Europe in places as far apart as the great arcaded courtyard wall of Crichton Castle, Midlothian (c1590) and the Palace of Facets in Moscow's Kremlin (c 1490). The shape of the openings is important at this time for the planters largely forsook the pointed medieval arch (except in some churches where the style was still considered appropriate) in favour of the round arch or the square-headed opening. The doorway of the old church beside Galgorm Castle, Co. Antrim (early 17th Century) is a good example of the new fashion with finely cut mouldings.

Left: *Derrygonnelly Old Church door, Co. Fermanagh (1623)*

PLANTATION CHURCHES

Above: *Tullynakill Church, Co. Fermanagh (1639)*

Left: *Tullynakill Church, Co. Fermanagh (1639)*

PLANTATION AND RENAISSANCE

Above: *The White House, Ballyspurge, Co. Down (1634)*

GABLED STRONG HOUSES

Even before the troubles of the middle of the century the basic character of houses was changing. Tower houses like the Bangor Custom House (1637) continued to be built, repaired and enlarged, but the lower, less defensible gabled house was also becoming more common. Among the earliest surviving examples is the White House, Ballyspurge on the Ards peninsula, which while retaining thick walls, pistol loops, bawn and a small gatehouse, has as its dominant characteristic the tall gable ends. The other White House, north of Belfast, is rather more cautious, retaining defensive towers at the front corners and only small windows on the ground floor. Other examples of defended gabled houses are found at Doohat, Co. Fermanagh, and Wray Castle, Ballymore, Co. Donegal. Wray, built about 1611 for Tirlogh Oge O'Boyle, is also an example of an Irish landlord creating the sort of defensive home more usually associated with the planters. The house was surrounded by a battlemented bawn wall with a generous provision of gunloops

GABLED STRONG HOUSES

and square flankers. The main gate, perhaps not surprisingly in this remote part of the province, is still in the late Gothic style with a shallow pointed arch. The house itself was strongly built, of two main storeys and with attic windows in the gables. The entrance front had five bays of openings but irregularly arranged, and the front door was protected by a stone porch.

Below: *Wray, County Donegal (c1611)*

PLANTATION AND RENAISSANCE

DOUBLE-PILE HOUSES

Another house-type which emerged during the 17th Century and later achieved great popularity was the double-pile house. This in effect was a combination of two gabled houses built side by side with a thick central wall, often carrying the chimney stacks, which divided two sets of rooms. Galgorm Castle, built by Dr. Alexander Colville some time after he acquired the property in 1629, is an early example of the type, built astride a earlier bawn of 1619. It has three storeys over a basement, curvilinear parapets and thick rubble stone walls, characteristic of the 17th century, with a

Below: *Galgorm Castle, Co. Antrim (c1635)*

DOUBLE-PILE HOUSE

massive central spine wall supporting two chimney stacks. It was modernized in 1834 when the old windows with their diamond-shaped panes were replaced with sash windows. The front door was inserted during the 1850s, and at the same time the original heavy, dark-oak panelling in the house interior, much favoured in the 17th Century, was removed. Now there remains only the oak stair, with heavy, turned balusters and corner newel posts with large, round tops.

The house built at Newtownstewart, Co. Tyrone, by Sir Robert Newcomen and completed about 1620, although now very fragmentary, was evidently also of this type. Its main surviving south wall has three crow-stepped gables and a scattering of mullioned windows with hood mouldings. The use of brick for flue linings and chimneys is a feature which appears in Ulster's buildings at this time. Chimneys tend to get taller and more ornamental. The surviving one at Newtownstewart has the plan of an eight-pointed star. What is most significant about the house, however, is that it may have had no provision for defence. It was destroyed in 1698 and never rebuilt.

Left: *Newtownstewart, Co. Tyrone (c1620-21)*

PLANTATION AND RENAISSANCE

Right: *Richhill entrance front, Co. Armagh (c1670)*

Below: *Richhill (Isometric drawing M. Jope)*

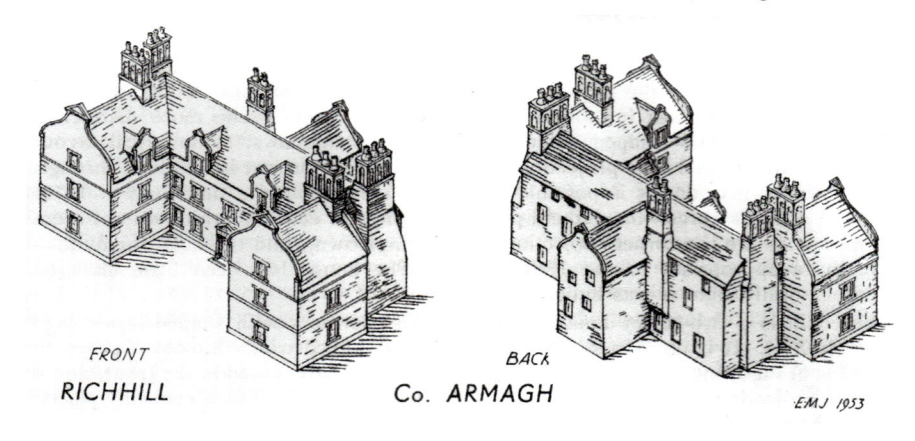

POST-RESTORATION HOUSES

Only after the wars of 1641-2 and the subsequent Cromwellian upheaval could the architecture of Ulster settle into a determined Classical progress. Richhill Castle, Co. Armagh (c1670) is among the earliest surviving houses to be designed almost completely without regard for defence. Its plan with a projecting staircase forming a basic inverted T-shape is a type which exists much earlier in England but continues in use through the 17th Century. Here the wings, placed somewhat like flankers, look back to a defensive tradition; but the rigid symmetry of the façade, the neat files of windows which are wide even on the ground floor, the tentative use of Classical details on the doorway, and the drama of the skyline, with its Dutch gables and regimented panelled chimneys, give the house a new Renaissance assurance. Waringstown, Co. Down, built in 1667, also has a regular fenestration, and was originally a two-storey house with end gables like those on Richhill. It subsequently acquired its present very imposing appearance by the addition of a third storey, flanking wings, and framing quoins and cornice. It originally boasted pedimented curvilinear gables and may have appeared very like Echlinville (Rubane), Co. Down, shown here on an early drawing.

POST-RESTORATION HOUSES

Above: *Waringstown House, Co. Down (1667)*

Left: *Echlinville (Rubane), Ards, Co. Down*

WILLIAM AND MARY HOUSE

It was not until after the Williamite wars that Ulster builders had a sustained opportunity to mature the local Classical tradition. A charming illustration of the caution with which the endeavour was carried out is Springhill, near Moneymore, built about 1698 by William Cunningham, a descendant of a planter family from Ayrshire. The central block with its high-pitched roof and solid chimneys at the gables is typical of the William and Mary period. So, too, are the rather tall, thin windows which betray, in the irregularity of their size and placing, the builder's uncertain handling of a Classical façade. The low wings with canted bays were added (c1765) to provide larger rooms. Together with the flanking buildings with curved gables, which are as old as the house, they counteract the central nervousness with a certain Baroque assurance which is greatly reinforced by the surviving early layout of the grounds with an axial drive running straight to the front door.

The rear elevation is now much more relaxed with the original tall central gabled staircase projection being imbalanced by other gabled additions. In its overall layout Springhill anticipates Georgian houses with linked wings but perhaps its nearest cousins are contemporary plantation houses in America.

Springhill, Co. Londonderry. Entrance front (c1698)

*Springhill, Co. Londonderry.
Upper floor of main staircase
(c1698)*

PLANTATION AND RENAISSANCE

Above: *Middle Church, Upper Ballinderry, Co. Antrim (1668, altered 1896)*

BARN CHURCH

Few churches of the later 17th Century remain in Ulster. The Middle Church at Upper Ballinderry built for the celebrated Jeremy Taylor (who, however, died before its consecration in 1668), was heavily though quite carefully restored in 1896 and still gives a clear idea of the type. Rectangular, with a simple gabled roof, the church looked much like a barn, and the type eventually achieved that nickname. External embellishments were minimal. At the west end a small bellcote houses the single bell. To one side an external flight of stairs gives access to a

BARN CHURCH

low gallery. The windows made of files of bulls-eye panes set in wooden frames give only limited light to what turns out to be a surprisingly rich interior with pews and doors of Irish oak, and a double-decker pulpit topped by a canopy sounding board. No doubt the influence of contemporary meeting houses resulted in churches remaining as simple as this until the early 19th Century, with a few startling exceptions like the Palladian Knockbreda (1737) and the Gothick opulence of Hillsborough (1760-74).

Below: *Lisbane Roman Catholic Chapel, Ardkeen, Co. Down.*

Vernacular Houses

Not everyone, however, was living in castles or large houses. On the contrary most people lived in much more humble dwellings; for alongside the growth of the Classical tradition in Ulster there developed the vernacular architecture; that is the native building carried out by local people using traditional methods and materials. Apart from a few descriptions and views on early maps little is known about local building until the end of the 17th Century. The traditional materials were stone, sometimes supplemented with turf for the walls, and thatch for the roof. The early cabins were on the whole small, badly lit and ventilated, liable to leak, and therefore wretchedly uncomfortable. Thatch survives best when kept dry from beneath so the placing of hearths and

Below: *Hezlett House, Liffock, Co. Londonderry (c1690)*

VERNACULAR HOUSES

burning of turf fires were vital considerations. From the 18th Century it is possible to follow the introduction of refinements, and to distinguish between the types in various localities. Hezlett House at Liffock, Co. Londonderry is an early example of the cruck-built house with gables of stone and turf reinforced with wooden crucks or crutches. It has also the gable ends with chimney stacks and direct access to the room space which are characteristic, very broadly speaking, of the north and the west of the province. In the south and east the fireplace tends to be in the middle of the house, screened from the entrance and lobby by a jamb wall; and the thatch is frequently hipped at the ends, making a roof with four surfaces. The development of the two types has sometimes been explained by variations in the housing of animals. Where there was a tradition of people sharing the same space as their domestic animals, especially milking cows, the open access arrangement was necessary. Where that tradition had disappeared (or never existed) the advantages of defending against draughts could be developed. Windows in both types were originally very small. The windows and fanlight of the Hezlett House are later insertions probably dating from about 1820.

Below: *Dromore, County Tyrone*

PLANTATION AND RENAISSANCE

Planter's House

Vernacular architecture could take rather grand forms. Almost exclusive to the areas where English plantation was predominant are the two-storey thatched houses, generally referred to as yeoman's or planter's houses. Unlike the single-storey 'long houses' which are never more than a single room wide, the planter's house could often be on a fairly large scale, as at Berwick Hall, near Moira, with its high-pitched roof and tall chimneys. Size alone, however, connects such buildings with the tradition of designed architecture. The materials, stone, thatch, rendering and whitewash, and the unorganized irregularity of the façade, all place the house firmly within the vernacular tradition. Sometimes the later attentions of architects can transform such a house into a more regular form, as appeared to have happened at Waringstown House. Here its vernacular origin results

Below: *Berwick Hall, near Moira, County Down (c1682)*

in the Classical decoration of the front door rather crowding the neighbouring windows. Somewhere between these extremes is such a house as Ballyvester, Donaghadee, Co. Down. Apparently built in the 1660s, it was remodelled about 1715 with five bays of windows with exposed sash boxes typical of this time. To get the bays regular three of the nine windows had to be painted dummies.

The Grange at Waringstown had a similar development which, thanks to dendrochronology (tree-ring dating), can be precisely dated. Timbers still in the house were cut in 1658 and 1692. The rubble stone front of the house suggests that it was originally single-storey. The house may then have had a thatched roof supported on timber crucks or couples. It seems that these timbers were re-used when the house was rebuilt with a slate roof and, perhaps, a more regular front in 1692.

Below: *Crookedstone, Co. Antrim (1699)*

The Eighteenth Century

THE EIGHTEENTH CENTURY

Previous Page: *Entrance to St. John's (C of I) Church, Moira, Co. Down (1723)*

Below: *Buncrana Castle, Co. Donegal (1716-18)*

EARLY GEORGIAN COUNTRY HOUSES

By contrast with Waringstown House or Berwick Hall, Buncrana, Co. Donegal, built by Sir John Vaughan between 1716 and 1718, is a competent and assured piece of architectural design; it may indeed be found rather dull because of this. Each window balances another. Each has its own area of wall to occupy, neither too large nor too small. The introduction of a half-basement raises both the height and the importance of the ground floor. The front door is approached by a gentle flight of narrowing steps, and decorated with a moulded frame topped by a curving open pediment. The three central bays are given

EARLY GEORGIAN COUNTRY HOUSES

a discreet prominence by being advanced slightly from the main block of the house, and the monotony of the blank side walls of the wings is relieved by the arched niches. A similar arrangement is present at Inch House on nearby Inch Island, and the simpler Linsfort Castle (1720) on Inishowen. A proposal for a house at Crum, Co. Fermanagh, c1716, has close parallels to Buncrana, though here there are also Franco-Scottish features, such as a central horseshoe staircase and arcaded terrace. The elements of design employed at Buncrana, those of balance, harmony and careful decoration are those which characterize the main course of Classical architecture in Ulster for the following century.

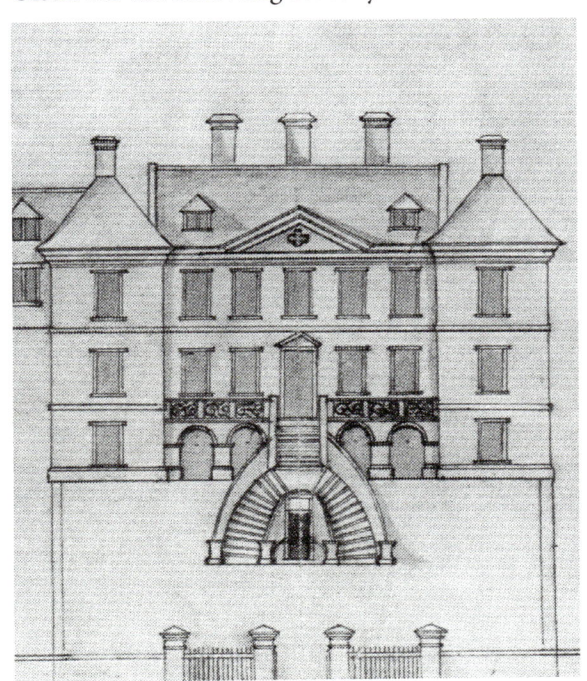

Above: *Crom (Crum) Castle, Co. Fermanagh. Proposal, c1716*

Right: *Buncrana entrance*

THE EIGHTEENTH CENTURY

Most of Ulster's 18th-Century building was not abreast of British fashions. In many cases there is a time lag of several decades before a fashion reaches remoter parts of the province. Two houses in Donegal demonstrate an extreme of this conservative tendency. Oakfield, the former Deanery at Raphoe (1737) and its close cousin, Bogay, near Newtowncunningham, have squat plans, chimneys rising from side walls, and raking, hipped roofs set with rows of dormers. The simple Classical doorways have triangular pediments supported on simple pilasters. In England they could be mistaken for houses built in the reign of William and Mary or even earlier. In Ulster they give themselves away by finely detailed woodwork and delicate stair fittings. The general external restraint, and the dominant relationship of wall to windows, might also suggest a small measure of influence from more stylistically advanced buildings of the time.

The first house at Castle Coole (now known only from drawings dated 1709) was an earlier but larger house with as sophisticated a design as any in Ulster at the time. The three central bays of the seven-bay front were set forward with quoins (corner stones) and topped with a triangular pediment. The arched front doorway had its own curved pediment supported on columns. All the windows had frames and on both floors their tops were linked with moulded string courses. The whole elevation was frames with quoins and a deep eaves cornice. The symmetry extended to roof dormers and chimneys and even to the side elevations.

Right: *Bogay, Newtowncunningham, Co. Donegal (c1730)*

EARLY GEORGIAN COUNTRY HOUSES

Left: *Oakfield House, Co. Donegal (1737)*

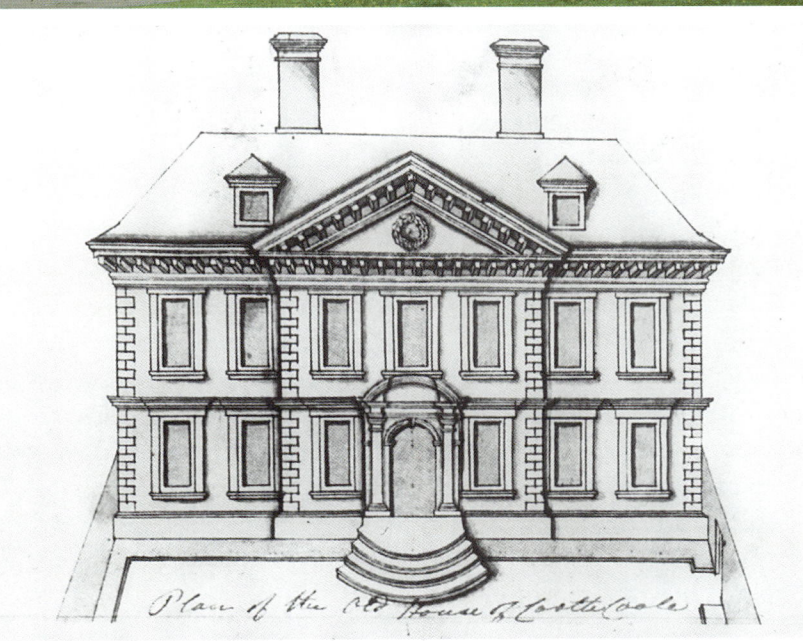

Left: *Castle Coole, Co. Fermanagh. Front elevation of the Queen Anne House by John Curle, 1709.*

THE EIGHTEENTH CENTURY

Above: *Prehen, Co. Londonderry (c1740)*

Usually, however, external decoration was confined mostly to entrance fronts – and mostly to the centre of these. An elaborate doorcase perhaps with more decorative windows above became a common theme for Ulster houses until well into the 19th Century. Two houses built just a few years later than Bogay demonstrate the development. Prehen (about 1740) near the town of Londonderry, now without its external render, has a rusticated doorcase formed by grouping the door and the two flanking windows into a single composition, the door itself being surmounted by a deep pediment. Port Hall (1746), Co. Donegal is a rarer example of how the repetition of a decorative feature, window frames interrupted with wide blocks, could be used to dramatic effect. Both seem to have been designed by Michael Priestley a local architect-builder who knew how to adapt pattern book designs.

Elaborate internal decoration of this period is rare, and its survival even rarer. At Red Hall, near Ballycarry, Co. Antrim, a complicated house with 17th-Century origins, there are plasterwork ceilings with compartmental circles, intersecting or framed with flowers. These look Jacobean at first sight yet they include female and male figures wearing early Georgian clothes.

EARLY GEORGIAN COUNTRY HOUSES

Above: *Porthall, Lifford, Co. Donegal (1746, Michael Priestley)*

Left: *Red Hall ceiling, Co. Antrim*

THE EIGHTEENTH CENTURY

Above: *Hall Craig, near Ross Lough, Co. Fermanagh (1721)*

EARLY GEORGIAN DOORS

Until the 19th Century (and by comparison with other countries even then) Ulster's buildings are rarely extravagantly decorated and never over-ornate. What had been a need for economy became in time an aesthetic preference. This perennial distrust of the showy is particularly marked in the external treatment of buildings. Yet while general embellishment does not occur, there was clearly a demand for local decoration some of which reaches a high standard. The carving of early Georgian stone doorways, for example, even in some most unlikely situations is particularly good. The modest house of Hall Craig, in Co. Fermanagh, boasts an open-pedimented doorcase carved in a most lively manner and quite as good as that at Buncrana. The segment-pedimented doorway at Antrim Court House is another fine example with crisp Classical detail enriched with floral garlands.

Even more elaborate was the doorcase at Gill Hall, Co. Down – alas, demolished now – which was a more sculptural version of the Antrim door with fully-rounded attached columns supporting a Classical entablature with a decorated frieze and a deep segmental pediment. Yet this aedicule, or framework, is only a setting for the doorways itself; its segment-headed, moulded frame is interrupted by large projecting square blocks and topped with a larger triple keystone. In the spandrels (corner spaces left between the top of the door and the Classical frame) dolphins wrestled in seaweed scrolls. The close relationship between this doorway and those at Antrim Court House (1726) and St. John's Church, Moira

EARLY GEORGIAN DOORS

Above left: *Door to Antrim Court House, Co. Antrim (1726)*

Above right : *Gill Hall doorcase, Co. Down (c1731, demolished)*

(1723; see p94) suggests that Gill Hall may have been the work of the same master masons; the blocking decoration around the doorway might suggest a slightly later date (see pp94-5).

THE EIGHTEENTH CENTURY

EARLY GEORGIAN PUBLIC BUILDING

Ulster's 17th-Century public buildings are known to us only from sketches and descriptions. Some, like those already mentioned at Londonderry (p63) were quite impressive; others appear to have been plain but functional. In these circumstances, the survival of Antrim Court House, one of the earliest and most poised of Ulster's public buildings, is a striking surprise. The work of an unidentified architect, this design - with boldly arcaded façades, emphasised corners, ornate cornice and deep eaves - has a rare poise which subsequent alterations and additions, with the honourable exception of the lantern of 1817, have not always respected. Surprisingly, perhaps because it was too sophisticated, the building found no obvious imitators, though its finish of painted stucco rendering, which is

Below: *Antrim Court House, Co. Antrim (1726)*

EARLY GEORGIAN PUBLIC BUILDING

possibly later than the original building, was to become the most popular treatment for houses in Georgian Ulster.

Twenty years later than Antrim, and just as imposing is the Court House at Lifford, Co. Donegal, built to designs by Michael Priestley in 1746. Its walls are also built of rubble covered with rendering and its prominent corner stones, or quoins, also form an important part of the design. Otherwise, however, the building is quite different. The roof is now hidden behind a tall blank parapet (just like that at Port Hall; also designed by Priestley). Unlike Antrim, where the central part of each elevation is set back, here the three middle bays push forward and are emphasised by their own set of quoins. The main decoration is reserved for the openings. Here the windows and the doorway have the same prominent blocks interrupting the frames. The name applied to this decoration is 'Gibbsian' after James Gibbs, the Scottish architect who made it popular through his own buildings but more importantly through his *A Book of Architecture* published in 1728 which was specifically designed to help patrons living in remoter parts of the country who might have difficulty in getting architectural advice. Priestley seems to have known the book; certainly his front door with its assured triangular pediment is borrowed directly from designs for Gibbs's most famous church, St. Martin-in-the-Fields in London.

Left: *Lifford Court House, Co. Donegal (1746, Michael Priestley)*

THE EIGHTEENTH CENTURY

EARLY GEORGIAN CHURCHES

It is during the early Georgian period that the first consistent use of professional architects is found in Ulster. The resultant impact may be seen by comparing two churches. St. John's Church at Moira, Co. Down is little more than a barn church with a tower embraced in the west end of its rectangular plan. The carving of its Classical doorway is fine but it seems too large, and the way it pushes up into the window above is clumsily designed. By contrast the façade of Newtownbreda Parish Church seems serene and uncrowded. The triangular pediment of the doorcase, is echoed by that of the pediment of the main bay, and again by the line of the roof. The height and shape of the spire relate to the rest of the façade; and the interior is no plain rectangle but a complex space, almost exactly a double cube, with a chancel and semi-circular transepts all carefully proportioned. The designer of Moira remains unknown; Newtownbreda was the work of Richard Castle, then Ireland's leading architect.

Somewhere between the two in style but later than both in date is Holy Trinity Church, Ballycastle, Co. Antrim, built in 1756. The plan is unadventurous and the main decoration, again, is concentrated on the west elevation. This is all of carved smooth, or 'ashlar', stone. The lower elements are all carefully arranged about the severe, pedimented central door. The relation of the tower and spire is more sophisticated than at Moira with a balustraded parapet enlivening their juncture. The only rather odd feature is the Venetian window applied to the tower. Only its arched central section could be glazed because, towards the corners, solid building was needed to support the spire. This piece of architectural 'showing off' (by a good craftsman with a pattern book in one hand?) is not improved by the oversized clock face balanced on its keystone.

Left: *Moira Parish Church, County Down (1722-26)*

EARLY GEORGIAN CHURCHES

Above:
Holy Trinity Church, Ballycastle, Co. Antrim (1754-6)

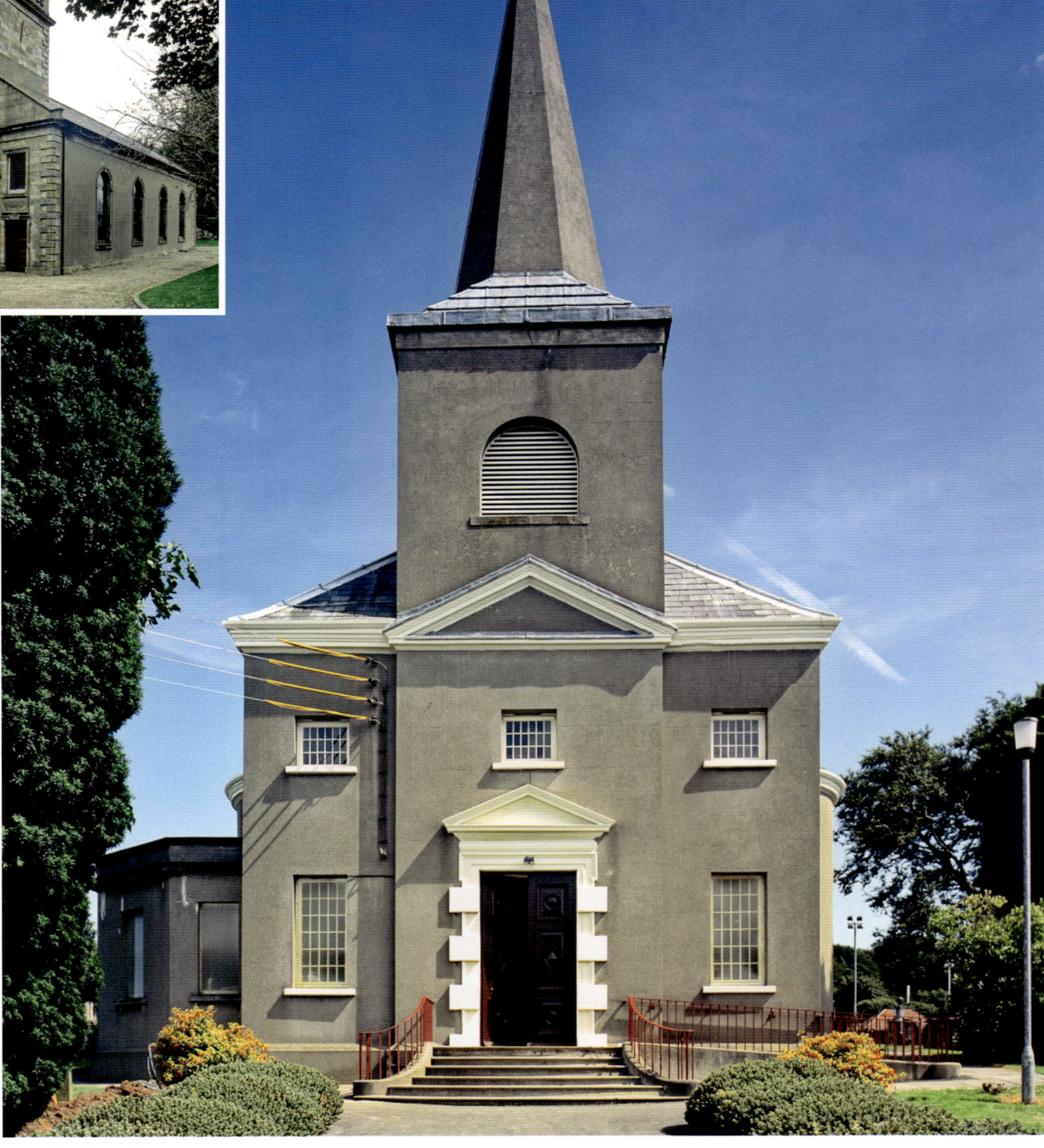

Right:
Newtownbreda Parish Church, County Down (Richard Castle, 1747)

95

THE EIGHTEENTH CENTURY

Above: *Drum Bridge Lock Keeper's House, Drumbeg, Co. Antrim (c1760, Thomas Omer)*

GEORGIAN ENGINEERING

Ulster building fashions may have lagged behind other parts of Britain and Ireland, but the same is not true of Ulster's engineering achievement in the Georgian period, which, far from being behind the times, actually led the way in Britain in canal development. The Newry Navigation built from 1731, the earliest inland canal in the British Isles, was controlled in succession by Sir Edward Lovett Pearce and Richard Castle. The Tyrone Canal, also planned in the early 1730s but, apparently, not under construction until the 1740s, was at one stage supervised by a Sardinian engineer, Davis Ducart. Slightly later Thomas Omer and Christopher Myers, were concerned with the ship canal from Newry to the sea (1754-69). The importance of all this engineering activity was that all these men, and there were others, were architect-engineers at a time when the professions were far from distinct. They all had experience of building fashions in England or on the continent; and eventually they would all contribute to the architecture of the Province. The architectural result of the influx of all these designers was significant; they brought about a new interest in the serious understanding and application of Classical design and they set the foundations for a local style which often had a strong engineering character. They were capable of grand schemes but they also showed how even small buildings can be treated as architectural designs. Among the best examples of this engineering work are the delightful lockkeepers' houses designed by Thomas Omer for the Lagan Navigation (c1760); just a few simple elements

GEORGIAN ENGINEERING

turn quite ordinary materials into a striking composition. Sometimes the design of buildings was entirely practical; their unadorned simplicity has an attraction of its own, especially when they have survived the rigours of time. Such is the case with Ballycopeland Windmill, Co Down, built in the 1780s and now (occasionally) the only working windmill in Ireland.

Right: *Newmills Aqueduct, Coalisland Canal, Co. Tyrone (Davis Duckart, c1760)*

Below: *Ballycopeland Windmill, Co. Down (c1785)*

THE EIGHTEENTH CENTURY

Above: *Saintfield House, Co. Down (c1750)*

MID-GEORGIAN COUNTRY HOUSES

Saintfield House, Co. Down, about 1750, a double-pile house with very plain elevations and windows set into large areas of wall, and minimal decoration represents the conservative character of much 'big house' building of the Mid-Georgian period. Leslie Hill, County Antrim, of the late 1750s, is much larger than Saintfield, but on its elevations equally restrained. What placed it into a grander category is that it once had balancing wings to each side of the main block housing kitchens and stables. This pattern derives from Italian villas and particularly from the example of Andrea Palladio in the countryside around Venice. The main block has three storeys over a basement and is seven bays wide. The windows are set in neat files; at each storey they are slightly shorter than those below. The three middle bays

MID-GEORGIAN COUNTRY HOUSES

project forward slightly to support a neat triangular pediment with a semi-circular attic window exactly the same width as the windows of the middle bay below. The front doorway has attached columns supporting entablature and pediment which are cut away to frame a semi-circular fanlight. Its proportions give it a central authority but it does not crowd its neighbouring windows. The roofs – it is another double-pile house – are regimented with balancing chimney stacks. The overall impression is of restraint and logic.

Below: *Leslie Hill, Ballymoney, Co. Antrim (c1758)*

THE EIGHTEENTH CENTURY

Opposite: *Florence Court dining room*

Below: *Florence Court front façade, Co. Fermangh*

Quite a contrast to Leslie Hill is provided by Florence Court, Co Fermanagh, also reputedly dating from the 1750s, but possibly earlier. At first glance the house might appear to have a coherent design; actually it has distinct phases. The main block originally stood alone and was approached by a straight axial drive (like Springhill p74-75). This is still the best viewpoint because most of the external decoration is concentrated on the front façade. A variety of features, adapted from pattern books, are gathered together heedless of whether they relate well to each other or to the whole design. Leslie Hill has one basic type of window; Florence Court has seven including those embraced by the wide door frame. The centre is particularly crowded with openings of varied sizes little related to those above or below. Although the three central bays break forward the effect is rather neutralised by the tall balustraded parapet which obscures the roof. The intention, no doubt, was to be impressive but the result, on closer inspection, is a charming muddle.

Very different are the wings, added after 1767. Arcades with rusticated pilasters stretch out to octagonal pavilions which are embellished with sculpture niches and pediments. These additions provide a sophisticated bolster to the assurance of the house. No such assistance is needed inside the main block where, so rare in Ulster, fine joinery is complemented by wonderful displays of Rococo plasterwork, possibly the work of the Dublin stuccodore, Robert West.

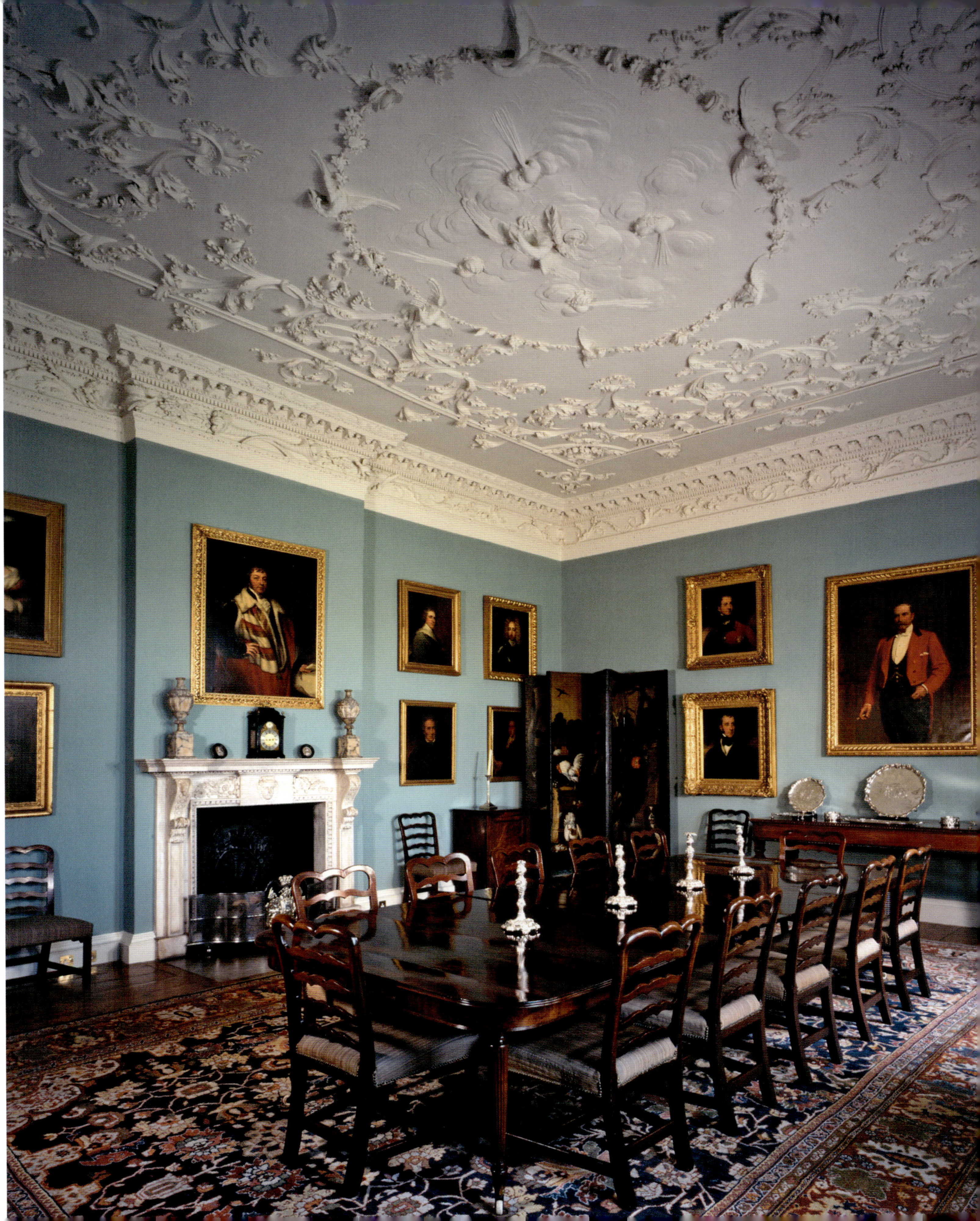

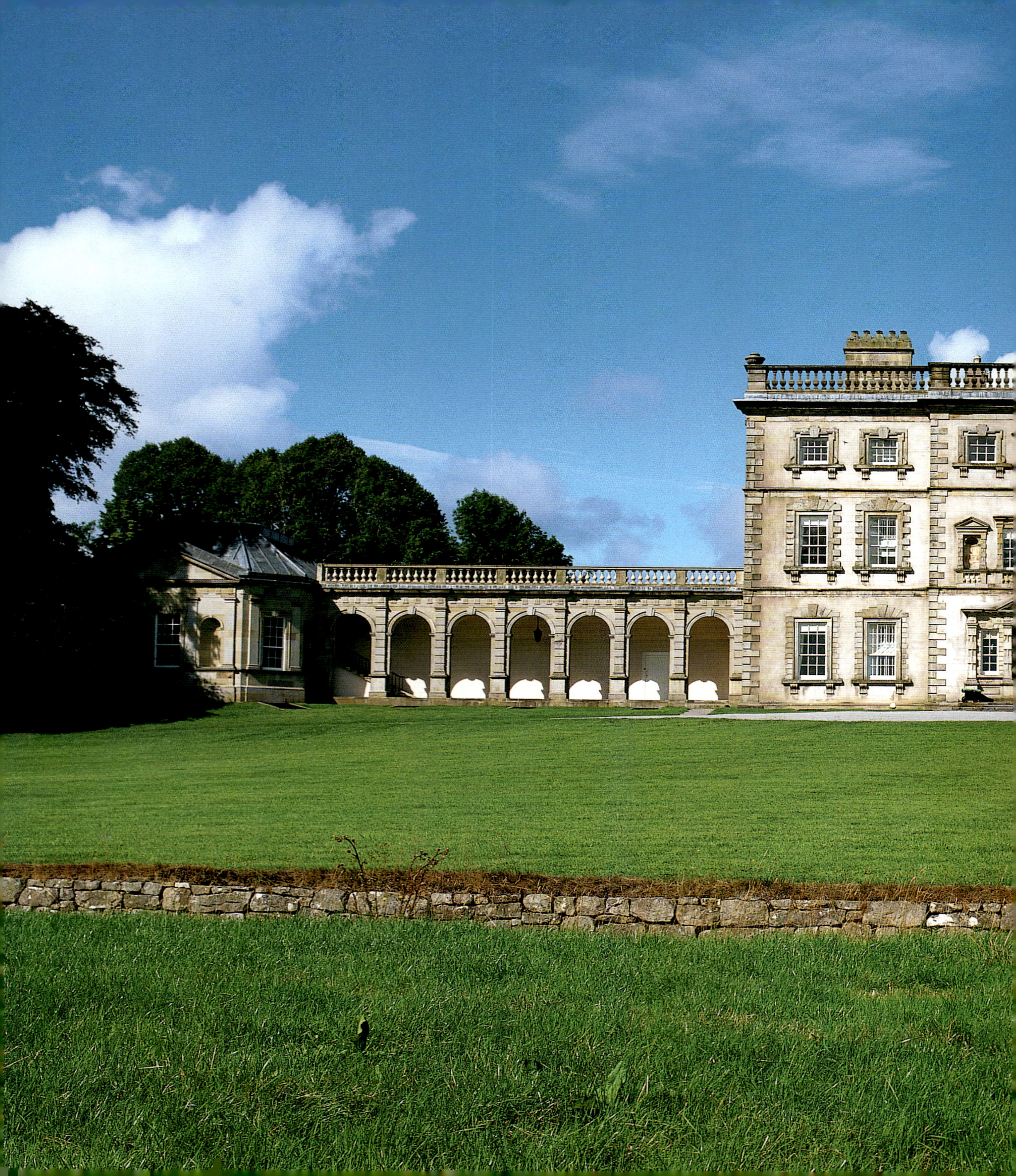

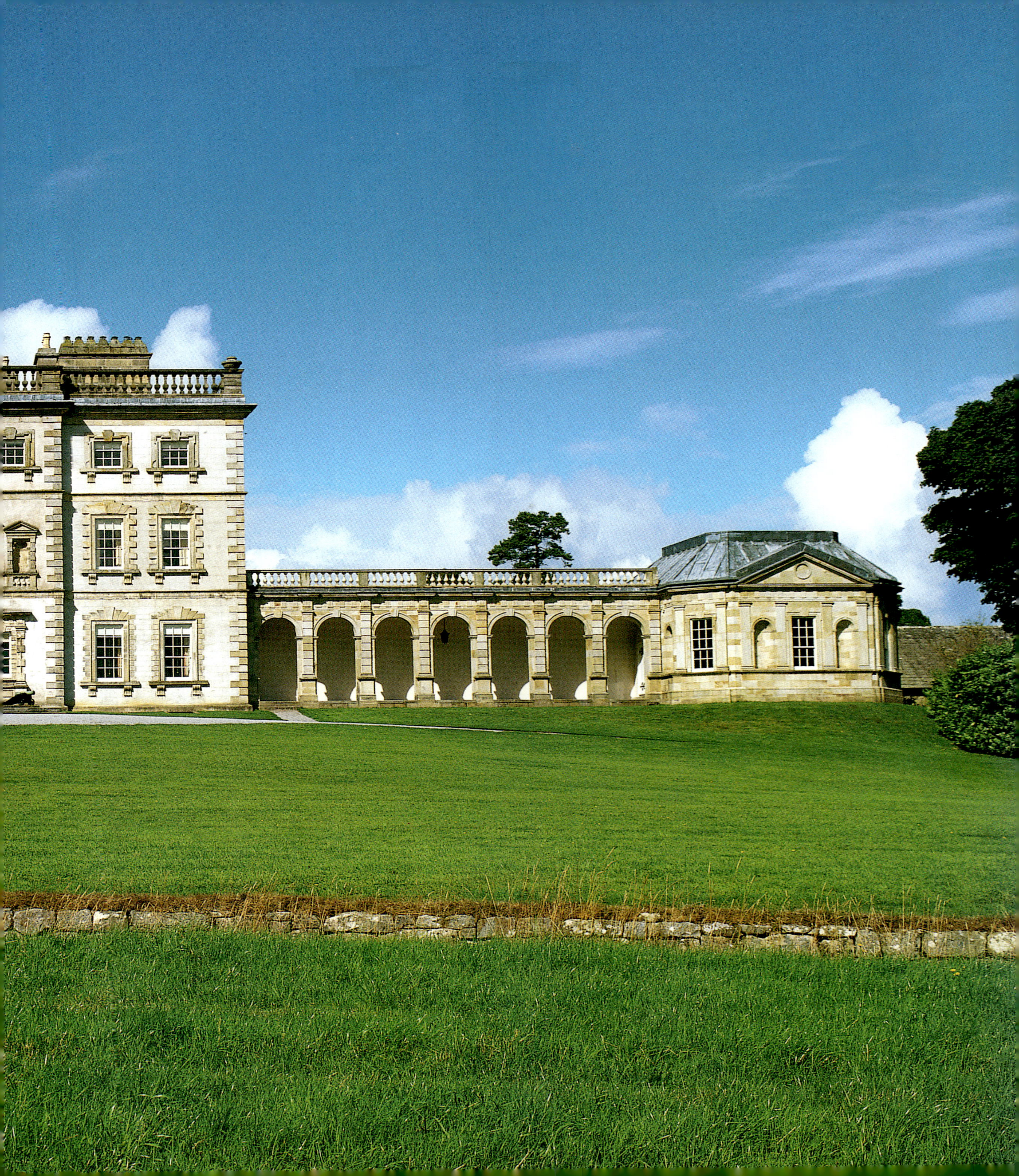

THE EIGHTEENTH CENTURY

Above: Bellamont Forest, Co. Cavan. Front Façade (Sir Edward Lovett Pearce, c1730)

Previous Pages: Florence Court, Co. Fermanagh. Front elevation.

PALLADIANISM

The Renaissance buildings of the humanist and theorist from Vicenza, Andrea Palladio (1508–80), began to influence English architecture during the 17th century. In the early Georgian period a second and more consuming interest in Palladio developed. One of the finest examples of a re-reinterpretation of Palladio's Villa Rotonda at Vicenza is Bellamont Forest, near Cootehill, Co. Cavan. It was erected around 1730 by the great Irish architect, Sir Edward Lovett Pearce (c1699-1733) and is composed of brick with a rusticated basement and has a large pedimented Doric portico dominating its five-bay front. The upper storey is treated as an attic, above a cornice, while the side elevations have Venetian windows. Inside, the hall boasts a high coved ceiling with a modillion cornice, with the walls below decorated with roundels for busts.

PALLADIANISM

Right: *Bellamont Forest – hall (c1730)*

THE EIGHTEENTH CENTURY

Richard Castle was an Italian-German engineer associated with the Palladian group in England. He came to Ireland possibly as an assistant to Sir Edward Lovett Pearce and was influenced by his mature Palladian style. His first known work was Castle Hume, County Fermanagh, (c1725), and although only the stables survive it is clear even from the quality of these that Castle was already an accomplished architect working in a Palladian vogue. The style which he introduced is easily identified by rather small windows (more appropriate to bright Italian sunshine than in the north) especially those nearest the eaves lines, set in wide areas of wall. He used also the doorways

Vicar's Hill, Armagh, Co. Armagh (1742)

PALLADIANISM

Above: *Southwell Charity, Downpatrick, Co. Down (1733)*

with alternate wide and narrow blocks of stone, a style called 'Gibbsian' after James Gibbs, the Scottish architect who pioneered it. Castle's influence on Ulster building is pronounced. Houses, like the Vicar's Hill Terrace, Armagh (1742 and later), and stable blocks, like those at Roe Park, Limavady, Co. Londonderry (c1740), show clearly that both the severity of Palladianism and the more decorative style of Gibbs were admired and imitated. The Southwell Charity, Downpatrick, Co Down (1733) is a good example of Palladian design with centre and wings and flanking teachers' houses.

THE EIGHTEENTH CENTURY

GEORGIAN GOTHICK

By the middle of the 18th Century the romantic writings and no less romantic building activities of Horace Walpole and others had resulted in a fashion for dressing houses in thin medieval garb. This style, called 'Gothick' to distinguish it from real medieval Gothic (and its 19th-Century revival) was first used in Ulster as a style for garden buildings like the eyecatcher at Greyabbey, or the series of follies at Tollymore Park, County Down. It was not long, however, before the country mansion acquired this whimsical, attractive manner from the smaller buildings in the demesne. An early and most remarkable example is Castle Ward, County Down, where, tradition states, the differing tastes of Lord Bangor and his wife resulted in a curiously divided house with

Below: *Castle Ward, The Gothick façade, Co. Down (1759-67)*

one side in the Classical Palladian style, with triangular pediment supported by columns raised on a rusticated ground floor, and the other side Gothick with pointed windows, battlements and parapet finial spikes. The division extends indoors with half the house enjoying Classical Rococo decoration and the other plunged in frivolous gloom with pointed doors and plaster vaulting.

Below: *Castle Ward, The Classical façade, Co. Down*

THE EIGHTEENTH CENTURY

Right: *Dunminning Cottage, Glarryford, Co. Antrim (c1810)*

The Gothick style was confined neither to houses nor great estates, though because of the expense it involved, it found its most satisfying results in the hands of lavish patrons. Just such a man was Wills Hill, who in his thwarted attempt to have Hillsborough created the county town of Down, erected two of the province's best Gothick buildings. The Fort (c1760) is a remodelling of the gatehouse of the artillery fort built about 1650, which is still substantially intact. The new gatehouse is a charming mock castle with pointed windows, paper-thin walls, and snap-off battlements. Even more impressive is the Parish Church (1760-1774), undoubtedly Ulster's finest Gothick church. Pointed and spikey with spire and finials outside and plaster and woodwork within, its rigid symmetry yet shows it to belong firmly in the Classical Georgian tradition, and this feeling is well emphasised by the long, straight approach up the avenue of limes from the twin Gothick lodges and gates on Hillsborough main street. But there are smaller and later examples which have great charm of their own. Dunminning Cottage, Glarryford, Co Antrim, apparently built about 1810 to house the toll-keeper for the bridge, is a charming example of the use of traditional materials made 'Gothick' simply by the pointed shape of its door and windows. The little manager's house at Spa, near Ballynahinch, was apparently built in an intentionally old-fashioned style early in Victoria's reign, but is no less delightful for that.

Below: *Hillsborough Fort Gatehouse, Co Down (C. Myers, c1760)*

THE EIGHTEENTH CENTURY

Above: *Ardress House, near Loughgall, Co. Armagh*

Gentleman's Farmhouse

As has been noticed with Waringstown House (pp12-13), some of Ulster's most unusual and interesting buildings are those which have developed over the centuries. The centre of the present house at Ardress dates from about 1660 and is a typical double-pile farm house of that period. Almost exactly a hundred years later the heiress to the property, Sarah Clarke, married George Ensor, a Dublin architect. Eventually, around 1780, they retired to the house and carried out extensive remodelling to turn the house into a gentleman's residence. It appears that George did not consider the front of the existing house to be sufficiently impressive; so he added two bays of windows at each end of the façade, including the tri-partite ones then in fashion. This exercise seems a little ludicrous when it is discovered that of the eight windows which he added five were dummies. But it was a great success for it allowed a second front with curving wings to be formed at right angles to the main façade, enjoying a different vista of country to the west. Inside the house is yet another surprise, a drawing room decorated by Michael Stapleton the Dubliner who excelled at the type of restrained, Neoclassical plasterwork with which Robert Adam was at that time superseding the swaying excesses of Rococo compositions.

GENTLEMAN'S FARMHOUSE

Left: *The Drawing Room, Ardress House, Co. Armagh (c1780, Michael Stapleton)*

Gentleman's 'Vernacular'

Alongside the more self-conscious architectural developments flourished the native traditions of stone and thatch. Occasionally the two traditions merge into a picturesque, Georgian 'vernacular' style which is Ulster's alone. Clady Cottage, Dunadry (c1780) is typically attractive with wide sash windows and pretty fanlight, but the regular spacing of windows, the balanced façade and the symmetrical planning show that this is self-conscious design rather than real vernacular building unaffected by stylish trends. Undoubtedly the most ambitiously developed example of the type is the house built around 1780 by Isaac Corry at Derrymore, near Newry, in County Armagh. Adopting both traditional ma-

Below: *Clady Cottage, Dunadry, Co.Antrim (c1780)*

terials and 'architectural' features like quatrefoil windows topped with label mouldings, the building is arranged as a series of small units round an open court. Thus the individual parts retain the modest scale of Ulster vernacular building yet the overall conception is rather grand. The first house at Blessingbourne, Fivemiletown, County Tyrone (now replaced) was handled in a similar manner, and another less ambitious example is Burrenwood Cottage, near Castlewellan, County Down. Rather later a more assertive picturesque style was introduced under the influence of the Regency architect John Nash; the result was a number of highly ornate houses in the cottage style, especially in the area around Rostrevor, Co. Down.

Below: *Derrymore House, Bessbrook, Co. Armagh (c1780)*

Neoclassical

By the middle of the 18th Century the fashion for taking the Grand Tour on the continent, as part of a young gentleman's education, had resulted in an increased interest in the precise nature of Classical architecture. Hitherto the Classical tradition had developed in the north as a general distillation of antique ideas transmitted through the books of Renaissance theorists like Sebastiano Serlio (1475-1554) and Andrea Palladio (1508-1580). Now appeared new French and English studies of the Greek and Roman buildings themselves, and these books became patterns for the serious revival of antique types. Of principal importance to the development of Ulster architecture was the example of James 'Athenian' Stuart who, with Nicholas Revett, published in 1762 the first of what became an influential series of pattern books called *The Antiquities of Athens*. Stuart also designed the Temple of the Winds at Mount Stewart, a precisely detailed adaptation of the Temple of the Winds at Athens. With its simple severity and opportunities for elaborate local decoration, the Classical revival appealed to Ulster architects and patrons alike; it continued to dominate the main course of building development for almost half a century.

The works patronized by the extravagant and indulgent Earl Bishop of Derry comprised some ambitious examples of Neoclassicism. Employing a confusion of architects (he was not an easy pa-

Left: *The Temple Of The Winds, Mount Stewart, Co Down (1781-85)*

NEOCLASSICAL

tron) he decorated his demesne at Downhill, Co. Londonderry, with elaborately correct Classical buildings based on Roman originals. Of these the finest is the cylindrical, domed Mussenden Temple (1783) designed as a library and perched on the edge of a cliff, so that scholars might observe the forces of nature in comfort. His other house at Ballyscullion, a version of the Pantheon at Rome with wings, was soon dismantled but its great Corinthian portico survives on the front of St. George's Church in Belfast.

Right and below: *The Mussenden Temple, Downhill, Co. Londonderry (1783)*

THE EIGHTEENTH CENTURY

As with the Gothick, so the Neoclassical style first appeared in Ulster with small buildings. Temples like the very Palladian Lady Anne's Temple at Castle Ward (c1755) and those Hillsborough (early 19th Century) were used as garden ornaments. Altogether more sombre and severe is the Templeton Mausoleum (1789) at Castle Upton, Templepatrick; this is the only Classical building in Ulster designed by Robert Adam, the celebrated architect who gave his name to the discreetly delicate style of revived Roman Imperial decoration which he made popular. Although the present mausoleum is a much reduced version of the original scheme, it has the peculiar poise associated with Adam's work; Classical sarcophagi and urns, leafy swags, circular reliefs, and exqui-

Below: *The Templeton Mausoleum, Castle Upton, Co. Antrim (1789)*

NEOCLASSICAL

Above: Archbishop Robinson's Chapel Armagh, Co. Armagh (1781-86)

sitely carved Roman letters all blend into a harmonious whole. Just as scholarly was the work patronised by Primate Robinson in Armagh. In particular the chapel (1781-86) beside his palace is one of the most complete Neoclassical buildings in the country. Externally it is essentially a temple with an archaeologically correct, tetrastyle (four-columned) Ionic portico supporting a pediment, and the pediment dictating the shape of the roof. Inside the floor is of square flags of local limestone (sometimes called 'Armagh marble') with corners blunted with smaller chevrons of black Kilkenny marble. The oak furnishings, including the Archbishop's throne, are superb in both design and craftsmanship. Completing the Neoclassical atmosphere, Corinthian pilasters rise to a full entablature with a vaulted coffered ceiling above. When Thomas Cooley, the original architect, died in 1784 he was succeeded by Francis Johnston, a local man who went on to a distinguished practice in Dublin, the first Ulster architect to make his mark outside the province.

THE EIGHTEENTH CENTURY

Above: *Castle Coole, Enniskillen, Co. Fermanagh. (James Wyatt, 1790-98)*

NEOCLASSICAL MANSIONS

It was not long before the Neoclassical style was being used for large buildings. During the two or three decades which embrace the turn of the century country seats were either remodelled or rebuilt in the style. This was the case at Castle Coole, Co. Fermanagh, where the Queen Anne house was entirely removed and James Wyatt, adapting the designs of Richard Johnston, created one of Ireland's most serene and accomplished domestic temples. Unlike the classical Palladian front at Castle Ward, the portico runs the full height of the façade, with its starkly unadorned columns set firmly on the ground. The general composition of main block and wings running out to pavilions harks back to Palladian houses like nearby Florence Court (c1750; wings 1767) but the mood is entirely new. The fussy cut-stone decoration and lightly arcaded wings of Florence Court are replaced with large areas of smooth stone and wings with severe, baseless columns supporting straight architraves. John Soane's remodelling of Baronscourt (1790-4), sadly destroyed by fire soon after its completion, was an even more dramatic affair. Some other good examples include Caledon, Tyrone (1779), The Argory, Co. Armagh (1820); The See House at Kilmore, Co. Monaghan (1830s), Colebrooke, Co. Fermanagh (1825) and Seaforde, Co. Down (1816-20).

NEOCLASSICAL MANSIONS

Above: *Castle Coole, Enniskillen, Co Fermanagh.*

GEORGIAN CHURCHES

The extent to which the Classical tradition influenced the more humble buildings of the country can best be seen in the development of church building. St. John's Church, Lisnadill, Co Armagh (1782-3), was one of number (and the best preserved in original state) of churches built for Primate Robinson to standard designs by Thomas Cooley. It combines a simple Gothic hall, with gables which look like simple Classical pediments, and a rather thin tower with extremely slight diagonal buttresses at the corners. Pointed openings, and finials and battlements are mixed with horizontal string courses and a Classical cornice. There is no mistaking this for real medieval building; nor was that the architect's intention. This is the application of what were then considered appropriate Gothick features to an essentially Classical design. It is playful; sometimes it is even called 'toy Gothick'. By the end of the 18th Century a simple pattern of hall-and-tower had evolved which was to dominate local church design for the first thirty years of the 19th Century. The tower is placed against the middle of one wall (usually the west gable) of the hall.

Kilmore Church, Co. Down built in 1792, is a very typical example with rounded Gothick windows and spikey finials and battlements to the tower. Beneath the tower a simple Gibbsian doorway gives access to a straight central aisle leading to the altar beneath the east window. The only asymmetry results from the typical omission of windows on the north wall. The wooden fittings would originally have been contrast-

Left: *St John's, Lisnadill, Co Armagh (1782-83)*

ingly informal with box pews varying in size, and a simple off-centre pulpit. Frequently the box pews were replaced in the late Georgian period by more rigid ranges of bench pews, while Victorian additions, porches, vestries, and transepts often contrived to break up the Classical symmetry. (What is not typical about Kilmore Church is that, long redundant, it was rebuilt at the Ulster Folk and Transport Museum and rededicated in 1983.)

Below: *Kilmore Parish Church, near Crossgar, Co Down (1779)*

GEORGIAN MEETING HOUSES

Meeting houses of the preaching denominations had never favoured the longitudinal arrangement of the medieval church. They preferred instead to concentrate attention on a central pulpit. Plans varied in shape. The 'T-plan much favoured in Scotland was also frequently used in parts of Ulster where Scots settled (Downpatrick Stream Street, early 18th Century; Rademon,1787). The old Presbyterian church at Dunmurry (1779) has a simple rectangular plan but a very elaborate façade decorated in the Gibbsian style so popular in Ulster throughout the 18th Century. Oval plans are used to great effect at Rosemary Street, Belfast (by Roger Mulholland,1783) and Randalstown (1790) where the bold geometry extended

Below: *Non-subscribing Presbyterian Church, Dunmurry, Co. Antrim*

to a polygonal porch and cupola (1830) and circular minister's room and highly successful oval gallery windows (both in 1929).

The interior of Rosemary Street is particularly accomplished. The elliptical plan provides the orchestral setting for a series of subtly curved variations. Twin access passages enclose a central boat-shaped block of box pews. Corinthian columns appear from the outer pews to support a gallery with a neatly panelled serpentine front. Above the arched windows a series of small vaults reach out together to support the oval ceiling with its radial and circular plaster decoration. Despite all these gentle distractions the focus remains firmly on the pulpit, and the minister with the Bible, at one end of the oval.

Above: *Non-subscribing Presbyterian Church, Randalstown, Co. Antrim (1790)*

The Nineteenth Century

THE NINETEENTH CENTURY

Above: *Clandeboye, near Bangor, Co. Down (1801-1804)*

Previous page: *Detail of stonework on the Albert Clock, Belfast (1865)*

LATE GEORGIAN MANSIONS

A number of the characteristics distinctive of later Georgian houses can be seen at Clandeboye, near Bangor, Co. Down, designed by Robert Woodgate, formerly Sir John Soane's clerk of works at Baronscourt. The principal fronts of this house are placed not back-to-back, but at right angles, permitting a more informal plan. Unlike many other mansions of this period the portico is of a modest scale, not dominating the design; curves are introduced by recessing windows in arches. The result is the more relaxed style associated with the Regency. Later in the century there were various proposals to remodel and enlarge the house in the Jacobean manor, in the French chateau style and as a Scots baronial castle, but all these remained very largely unexecuted. The essential character of Woodgate's house was little altered.

A more austere mansion is Colebrooke in Co. Fermanagh. This is the result of the remodelling from 1819 by William Farrell of an earlier three storey house, the new part being only two but reaching to the same overall height. The typically enlarged scale of the Neoclassical house is focused externally on the full-height portico with free-standing columns – of the Greek Ionic order with 'ram's horn' capitals. The design uses running elements to bind the elevations together: an eaves cornice and string courses, one between the upper and lower windows, and a second one linking all the upper window sills. The aim is to be impressive; the unadorned formality of the exterior gives no hint of fine plasterwork and more relaxed atmosphere within.

Another severe but impressive ashlar-faced house is Seaforde, Co.Down. It was built in 1816-20 by the English architect Peter Frederick Robinson. Two other examples of this type of domestic Neoclassicism, both by William Vitruvius Morrison, of Dublin, improving on the work of English architects, were the rebuilding of Baronscourt (c1832; after the house designed by John Soane was destroyed by fire in 1796) and the extension of Mount Stewart (1835) an 18th-century house which had already been extended by George Dance the Younger (1804-5).

LATE GEORGIAN MANSIONS

Above: *Colebrooke Park, Co. Fermanagh (1819-25)*

Right: *Seaforde House, Co. Down (1816-20)*

Regency Architecture

John Nash, the Prince Regent's architect, contributed more than buildings to Ulster. He seemed to use the province as a practice ground. At Lissan Rectory, built for the Reverend John Staples in 1807, he produced an elongated Ulster variation on his English Italianate villa, Cronkhill, near Shrewsbury (1802). The house has an intentionally irregular outline with its entrance in a square tower and an arcaded loggia on the garden side; a long wing reaching out to a circular turret (which, however, has been removed). This informal external style so typical of the relaxation of Regency style in England seems to have had little appeal to the perennially stern Ulster outlook. By contrast, other early 19th-Century rectories, though comfortably planned within, have plain, square, even forbidding exteriors. Elements of Nash's other principal work, the remodelling of Caledon House, County Tyrone, did on the other hand make an impact. Thomas Cooley's house (1779) at Caledon which Nash remodelled (c1812) had the large, flat, rather monotonous façades so frequently repeated in mid-Georgian Ireland. Nash treated the principal front in the manner of his contemporary Regent's Park Crescent by running a coupled colonnade along the ground floor, and then flanking it with domed pavilions, The coupled columns recur frequently on less ambitious Ulster porticos; so, too, do the recessed arches and wide windows, which contribute so much to the curving playfulness of Regency design.

Some of the best Regency interiors in Ulster can be found in Castle Coole, Co. Fermanagh. The house remained incomplete when the first Lord Belmore died in 1802, but between 1807 and 1825 his son, the second Earl, carried out a major programme of interior decoration. He em-

Right: *Caledon House, Caledon, County Tyrone. Watercolour by G.S. Repton*

REGENCY ARCHITECTURE

ployed John Preston, the outstanding Dublin furniture maker and upholsterer, who worked in the most up-to-date Regency fashion. Such extravagant decoration was very unusual in Ulster and its survival is rare anywhere. Rooms coloured in subtle sequence have sets of gilded furniture in what was regarded as Greek style and tailored to the spaces. Colours are rich and the upholstery fine and fulsome. Elaborately swagged curtains have fringes and tassels brought to an art form.

Left: *Castle Coole, Co. Fermanagh. The Saloon (1816-17)*

The Picturesque

The rise of the Picturesque Movement at the end of the eighteenth century meant that designers increasingly sought variety and irregularity in design. The asymmetric Gothic castle style, pioneered by Richard Payne Knight at Downton Castle, Herefordshire, became a fashionable alternative to the Neoclassical house. The style was made popular by John Nash, whose large practice extended to Ulster on several occasions. His house at Kilwaughter (1807) is now ruinous, and Shane's Castle (c1812), also in County Antrim, was never completed, but Killymoon Castle, County Tyrone, built in 1803, is earlier and better than either. Unlike some of Nash's less reputable works it is all of cut stone with excellent carved details, while the irregular planning endows it

Below: *Killymoon Castle, Cookstown, Co. Tyrone (1803, John Nash)*

THE PICTURESQUE

with a series of greatly varied rooms and elevations.

Also popular in Ulster was the symmetrical castle, a type developed earlier by Robert Adam in Scotland. Adam himself remodelled Castle Upton (1788) in a style which, exceptionally, was not symmetrical and has had many later alterations. The least changed part of his work is the stable range and double courtyard which has a tower over the entrance arch and Adam's characteristic wide battlements, non-functional machicolations (defensive dropholes) acting as a cornice, and projecting bays ornamented with blind crossbow loops. The underlying control of the design is essentially Classical. Defensive features are used for decoration. There is something of the toy fort about the style – only less serious. Among the best local designs in the playful castle style are Henry O'Hara's castle at Portstewart (1834) now part of a school, and the more simple Dungiven Castle, Co. Londonderry (1839). Two in ruinous condition, both designed by J.B.Keane, are Necarne Castle, Irvinestown (c1825) which has a purely Classical interior, and Magheramena, near Belleek (c1838) both in Co Fermanagh.

Below: *Dungiven Castle, Co. Tyrone (1839, Stewart Gordon)*

Above: *Killevy Castle, Meigh, Co. Armagh (1836, George Papworth)*

CASTLE STYLE

Perhaps the most charming example of a patron's determination to make his house his castle is Killevy Castle in Co Armagh, designed by George Papworth of Dublin in 1836. Set on a hill with its main front seen from below, it has a convincing set of castle features. The symmetrical front block has a central entrance set in a buttressed polygonal tower. The wings have windows in deep 'Tudor' arches flanked with dummy bow slots and terminating with taller square towers. Behind, and breaking the symmetry, are two more towers, one square and the tallest round. There are battlements everywhere even on the revetment garden walls which, in views from the valley give the appearance of a curtain wall defending an outer ward. But the scale is small and views from further up the hill reveal that this is essentially a rectangular late-Georgian house, with a central bow and a tower plonked on each corner. The battlements of the central tower reach back only as far as the chimneys, and then stop giving the impression of a stage set not meant to

CASTLE STYLE

Above: Gosford Castle, Co. Armagh (1819-49, Thomas Hopper)

be seen from this angle. It is altogether a sham, unpretentious and fun.

The same can not be said of Gosford Castle at Markethill, Co. Armagh, which was designed by Thomas Hopper from 1819. Hopper was a fashionable Regency architect who, like many of the time, worked in a range of styles. His most original works were his two picturesque 'Norman' castles, Gosford and the slightly later Penrhyn in north Wales. Hopper was born in Rochester and made good use of his knowledge of the castle there. The general impression is picturesque with a series of ranges jumbled about a tall 'keep' and reaching out to remote towers – one a great drum. Unlike Nash's Killymoon, Gosford takes itself seriously with thick walls and details skilfully adapted from medieval originals. Altogether the castle shows a new, more scholarly approach to reviving the spirit of a building of the past; and in this it anticipates the earnest revival of styles for particular purposes in the Victorian period.

Neoclassical Public Building

With its echoes of ancient authority and power the Neoclassical style was much favoured for the design of public buildings in Ulster's towns during the early years of the 19th Century, It is also interesting to notice that, while architects were still employed from outside Ulster, an increasing number came from Dublin rather than Britain.

The fine courthouse at Londonderry (1816) was designed in the Dublin office of John Bowden, who was also responsible for St. George's Church, Belfast. Monaghan courthouse (1830) was the work of one of Bowden's pupils, Joseph Welland, who later, as architect to the Ecclesiastical Commissioners, gave Ulster several fine churches. Another Dubliner, John Hargrave, designed the good courthouses at Omagh (1820), Dungannon (1830), and Letterkenny (1831), as well as exe-

Below: *Armagh Court House, The Mall, Armagh (1809)*

cuting domestic works. The courthouses at Enniskillen (1821-2) and Cavan (1825) were designed by William Farrell yet another Dublin architect.

In the earlier and exceptional case of Francis Johnston the process was reversed. Born in Armagh, where he designed a series of distinguished Classical buildings, he later moved to Dublin and became the greatest Irish architect of his generation. His courthouse at Armagh (1807-9) is the most sophisticated in the province both inside and out. Its elegant portico presides over the north end of the Mall, the focus of one of the province's finest architectural assemblies.

Following the example set by Sir John Soane's designs for the Belfast Academical Institution which was founded in 1810, the city of Belfast took on a determined Classical aspect which resulted in it receiving the nickname 'The Athens of the North' in some contemporary journals. Looking about the city now it is difficult to believe that such a title could be meant or taken seriously. Yet that was perhaps the most attractive moment of the city's development; the two large squares were laid out and not cluttered with buildings of too large a scale, and the porticos of at least seven churches showed that the Classical Revival reigned supreme. The Old Museum Building, in College Square North, was designed by local men, Thomas Duff and Thomas Jackson, and opened in 1831. In the archaeological correctness of its features, especially the Temple of the Winds columns of its portico, it embodied in both style and function the spirit of the new enlightenment.

Right: *Old Museum building, College Square, Belfast (1830-34)*

THE NINETEENTH CENTURY

Faith Mission Hall, Ballymena, County Antrim (1845)

EARLY VICTORIAN CHURCHES

In the early years of Queen Victoria's reign church design pivoted uneasily between the late Gothick and late Classical styles. The Scotch Church in the Mall at Armagh (1837) has a complex Classical front with triangular pediment, full height pilasters, and other careful details such as the raking Greek window frames in the end bays of the first floor. By contrast the chapel now occupied as the Faith Mission Hall in

EARLY VICTORIAN CHURCHES

Ballymena (1845) has pointed openings, thin battlements and rather contrived buttresses; yet with its rigidly balanced front it, too, remains well within the broad Classical tradition. Following the shock of Cottingham's sweeping restoration of St. Patrick's Cathedral, Armagh, Ulster was generally not tempted until late in the 1840s to rush into the serious Gothic Revival then being preached by A.N.W. Pugin. With their long histories, the Episcopal churches, Anglican and Roman Catholic, were the first to explore the potential of reviving the forms and spirit of medieval church building. Understandably, resistance to this development was strongest among the evangelising sects. The first serious Gothic church for Presbyterians was built in Newry in 1853; the Methodists waited until 1865 at Portstewart.

Below: *Scotch Church, The Mall, Armagh (1837)*

THE NINETEENTH CENTURY

Above: Donaghadee Harbour Lighthouse, Co. Down (John Rennie, 1821-34)

VICTORIAN ENGINEERING

The spirit which placed Ulster in the forefront of engineering endeavour in the 18th century continued during the next century. The survival of Donaghadee harbour with its lighthouse (1821-34) is a wonder in itself. Designed by John Rennie and built from huge blocks of Anglesea limestone, it performed well as the Irish end of the short-sea passage used by the mail packets; but its partner, Portpatrick, facing prevailing winds on a jagged coast, could not. The post office service was transferred to Belfast in 1849, and the regular link with Donaghadee was abandoned in 1867. Never extended, remodelled or over-developed, the late-Georgian harbour remains in pristine form.

The once neglected and now cherished Palm House in the Botanic Gardens at Belfast is the earliest known construction by the celebrated Dublin ironmaster Richard Turner, whose later works included the Glasnevin conservatory (1842-50), near Dublin, and the great Palm House at Kew Gardens (1844-48), as well as consultation about the curved roof of Sir Joseph Paxton's Crystal Palace (1851). The wings of the Palm House at Belfast date from 1839-40, which, rather surprisingly, also makes them one of the earliest, surviving, substantial compositions of cast-iron and curvilinear glass in the world. The graceful central bulb was added to somewhat modified designs after 1852.

As an indication that other great engineering endeavours were afoot at this time it is relevant to notice that Turner was also responsible for the design of railway station roofs in Belfast, Dub-

VICTORIAN ENGINEERING

lin and Liverpool. Indeed many of the greatest structures of this time were related to communications. Improved roads and harbours, lighthouses, and the spreading railway network all presented challenges which engineers and contractors tackled with resolution and style. The Glendun viaduct of 1839 has a Roman grandeur, while the Egyptian Arch near Bessbrook, Co Armagh, carrying the railway over the Newry road, is fit for the passage of a pharaoh.

Above: *The Palm House, Botanic Gardens, Stranmillis, Belfast (1839-40 & 1852)*

THE NINETEENTH CENTURY

Above: *Ballywalter Park, Ards, County Down (1844-46)*

EARLY VICTORIAN MANSIONS: ITALIANATE

The Italianate style was generally seen as being a more relaxed and informal alternative to full-blown Neoclassicism. As the 19th Century progressed, the style was to become increasingly studied and adapted for modern use. This was partly because it offered flexibility but much more important were its historical associations. The fancy dress party of early Victorian architectural practice offered a bewildering choice. Soon styles were being used for very particular reasons. The association of the Italianate style was with the Renaissance princes of the 15th and 16th Centuries, and particularly with the merchants and bankers of Florence. (It is no accident that until quite recently the two shilling piece, even in its latest manifestation as a 10p coin, was known as a 'florin') These efficient businessmen, with agents all over Europe, developed commerce, encouraged the arts and sponsored scientific activity. And the greatest, such as the Strozzi, Rucellai and Medici achieved power and prestige. Along the way they sponsored architects to create a new architecture which, though imbued with the Roman past, had its own character combining practicality with a new logic and lightness. Here was a most suitable role-model for those whose wealth was derived from industry and commerce (rather than ancient landed estates and manorial rights) and wished to show that they could be

EARLY VICTORIAN MANSIONS: ITALIANATE

cultivated. In the heady days of Ulster's greatest period of expansion there were plenty who, consciously or unconsciously, would have felt comfortable with such associations. In Charles Lanyon they had just the right architect; he had first hand knowledge in both Sussex and London of the work of Sir Charles Barry then the leading exponent of the Italianate style. In his hands, and in those of many who imitated him, the Italianate style achieved immense popularity in Ulster – in houses of all sizes, and not just in houses.

Ballywalter Park, Co. Down (1844-46) built for Andrew Mulholland the proprietor of Belfast's York Street Spinning Company is one of the grandest examples of Lanyon's Italianate style, with heavy stucco embellishments to the principal windows, deep, bracketed eaves, and high, moulded chimneys. The exterior has an assurance which makes the addition of wings with bows, and even a long arm reaching to a domed conservatory, look entirely natural. The main rooms are ranged around a cavernous central stair hall. In Florence this would have been open to the sky with a fountain playing in the courtyard. Equally splendid is Dundarave, the home of the McNaghtens, near Bushmills, Co Antrim, Lanyon's other major palazzo. Unlike Ballywalter, it is not the remodelling of an older house and there is more coherence to its wholly two-storey elevations. Its central cortile is smaller because the staircase is not included, but the marbling of the arcades (in this case actually by Italians) is impressively rich.

Left: *Dundarave, Co Antrim (1847, Charles Lanyon)*

Above: *Glenarm Castle, Co. Antrim (1823-32, William Morrison)*

Early Victorian Mansions: Jacobethan

The most popular alternative to the Italianate was the revival of 16th- and 17th-Century English manorial architecture. To those with land (no matter how recently acquired) the idea of building a manor house had a particular appeal. There were several varieties on offer. The Tudor Revival reflected the last phase of medieval building, using the mullions and transoms of perpendicular building, the last and lowest of pointed arches, and a tendency to irregular planning. The Elizabethan Revival looked to more integrated planning, balanced façades, large areas of windows, often in bays, gathered chimneys, and even the appearance of Classical details. The Jacobean Revival could be more wholeheartedly Classical mixing Renaissance columns and cornices with earlier features. It could also incorporate north European Renaissance features such as flat 'strapwork' decoration, circular windows or shaped, curved gables. In Ulster, too, with its many Scottish associations, baronial bits could be used. Even a few Irish features such as tapering corbels and double-stepped battlements could get into the mix. With such an array of possibilities it is little wonder that architects, especially those less familiar with English originals, should get in a muddle. Although one phase usually predominates, there has been a tendency to give them the portmanteau name 'Jacobethan'. What they have in common is eventful walls, multitudes of labels, and skylines alive with finials, tall grouped chimneys, crenellated parapets, turrets and often one taller tower.

EARLY VICTORIAN MANSIONS: JACOBETHAN

Above: *Brownlow House, Co. Armagh (1838-42, William H. Playfair)*

Many fine examples are before or right at the beginning of Victoria's reign. Glenarm Castle (William Morrison, 1823-32) with its firmly regimented gables and corner domed turrets is still essentially Classical but contemporaries thought it 'Elizabethan'. It has a separate tower, actually a gatehouse commanding the bridge approach. Narrow Water Castle, designed by Thomas Duff of Newry was being built in 1836. Its gatehouse with four cupolas seems to derive from Hampton Court. With its asymmetrical layout and tall polygonal tower at one side, it is more 'Tudor'. Brownlow House (1838-42) was designed by the leading Edinburgh architect, William Henry Playfair, and again the studied irregularity of the plan suggests 'Tudor' but the sophisticated geometry of its plan makes it more 'Elizabethan'.

Above: *Narrow Water Castle, Co. Down (c1836, Thomas Duff)*

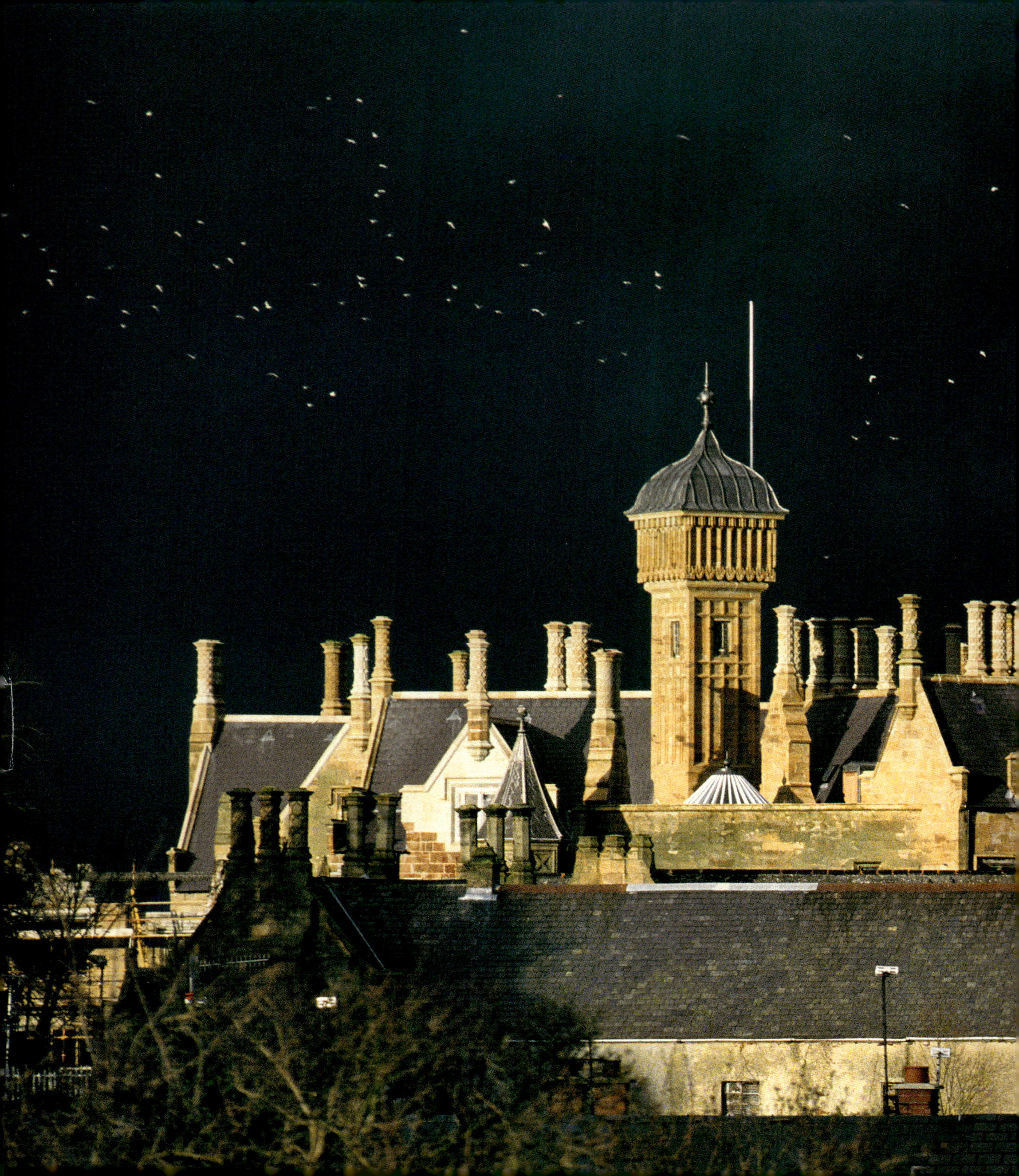

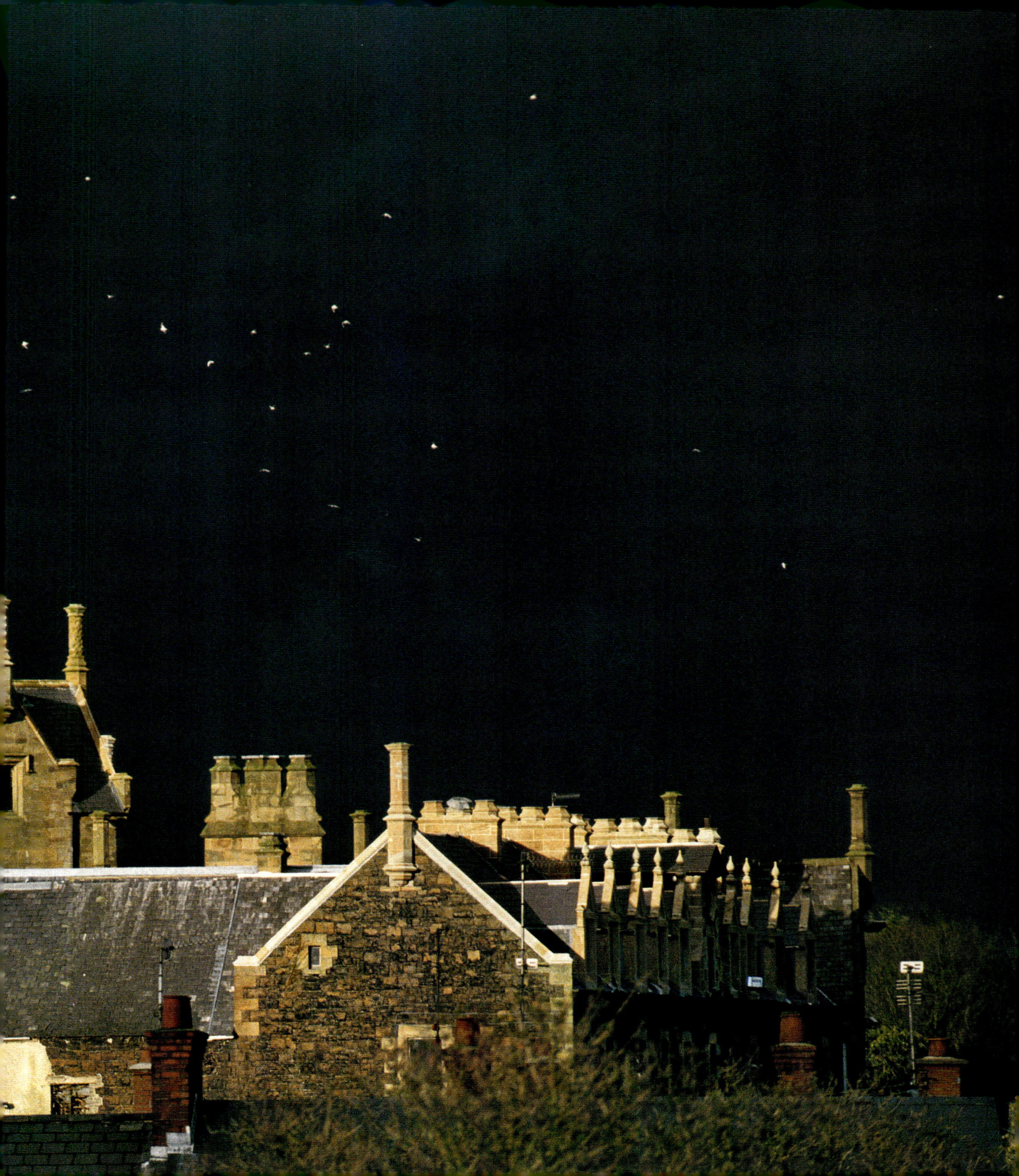

THE NINETEENTH CENTURY

Previous Pages:
*Brownlow House,
Lurgan, Co. Armagh
(photograph: T.Corry)*

*Methodist College,
Belfast (1865-68)*

ACADEMIC TUDOR

Early Victorians' choice of building styles for associational reasons went well beyond houses. The Regency demand for novelty had resulted in a great multiplication of available revivals. Victorians, generally less confident in matters of architecture and more keen to be seen doing the correct thing, chose associations as the easy way out. Thus, a gaol to be safe could look like a strong castle; a church to be pious must look medieval; a Turkish bath must have minarets, and so on. Undoubtedly one of the most successful revivals was that of the academic Tudor. The argument was simple; to look and function well as a school or college a building must appear like a real Tudor college, preferably with direct quotations from Oxford or Cambridge. Hence in designing the Queen's College in Belfast (1846-49), Charles Lanyon adapted freely and successfully from the details of the Founder's Tower at Magdalen College, Oxford. Now Queen's itself is comparatively old and its mellow brick façade rich with carved stone, diamond-pane windows, buttresses, battlements and finials, is one of the great architectural sights of Ulster. Later compositions in a similar vein include Magee College, Londonderry (1853-60), Methodist College, Belfast (1865-8), and the Belfast Academy (1879).

These, however, are only the grander examples. The Tudor style was also adapted and diluted for hundreds of Ulster schools, almshouses, and other institutions such as the Poor Law Union Workhouses (1839-1845; see Introduction) for which George Wilkinson produced both Tudor and Jacobean designs.

ACADEMIC TUDOR

Below: *The Queen's College, Belfast (1846-49, Charles Lanyon)*

THE NINETEENTH CENTURY

Italianate Banks

The architecture of banks plays an important part in the Victorian streetscape of Ulster. The general association, like that already noticed at Ballywalter, was with the wealthy families of 15th and 16th Century Italy, wealthy very often because they were bankers. The ornate stone front of the old Belfast Bank at Armagh (Charles Lanyon,1851) is an exceptionally vigorous example of Italian Mannerist revival. The windows and entrance doorway are embraced in a full-

Below: *Tourist Office - Former Belfast Bank, Armagh (1851)*

ITALIANATE BANKS

height rusticated arcade with lively sculpture and a heavy dominating cornice. The whole compositon may derive from the house that Giulio Romano built for himself in Mantua about 1545.

Closely related but even grander is Lanyon's Northern Bank (now Trustee Savings Bank), Victoria Street, Belfast (1851-2). This is even more Mannerist. The rusticated arcade runs across the front elevation which, however, is not in one plane. Wing bays advance with finely-carved window surrounds set into the rusticated arches. This leaves a slightly recessed centre which is treated as a triumphal entrance with the three arches set between two attached columns and two quarter columns. Once again the inspiration for full-height Tuscan Doric columns set against a rusticated wall may be Giulio Romano, this time at the Palazzo del Te built for Federico Gonzaga about 1530.

First Trust Bank (Northern Bank), Victoria Street, Belfast (1851-2, Charles Lanyon)

151

THE NINETEENTH CENTURY

HIGH VICTORIAN: RUSKIN'S INFLUENCE

Below: *Tesco (former Provincial Bank & Allied Irish Bank), Castle Place, Belfast (W. J. Barre, 1864-9)*

In admiring the architecture of northern Italy John Ruskin noticed its mixed quality; it mixed materials to give a dancing polychrome texture, and it also mixed the pointed Gothic tradition of the north with the solid, round-arched manner derived from antique Rome in the south. He saw the possibility of imitating this mixture as a way of breaking the boredom of what he considered to be the unnecessary limitation of quoting only one style at a time. The Newry man William Barre was principal among those who put Ruskin's theory into practice. His Provincial Bank in Castle Place, Belfast is an outstanding il-

HIGH VICTORIAN: RUSKIN'S INFLUENCE

lustration of what could be achieved. The basic classicism of the building can be readily identified by the symmetry and the central triangular pediment. Yet the decoration is medieval. The faces of hairy Lombard warriors look out from foliage beneath deep, rounded, Romanesque arches. Colonnettes flank the openings, and even the balustrade along the roofline is adapted from an interlacing Saxon arcade.

Right: *Tesco (former Provincial Bank), Castle Place, Belfast. Interior (1864-9)*

Below: *Stucco figure representing War in groin angle of dome (1869)*

153

Clarence Place Hall, Diocesan Offices,. May Street, Belfast (Lanyon, Lynn and Lanyon, 1865-7)

RUSKINIAN GOTHIC

Ruskin's admiration for the architecture of Venice and Northern Italy contributed much to the evolution of the mixed High Victorian style. One of the earliest instances of a building anywhere in the Venetian style is the Belfast (Northern) Bank at Newtownards (1854) and the bank at Dungannon (1855). Here all the windows group together in the middle of the façades just like those of Venetian Palaces along the canal fronts.

By the middle of the 1860s the general use of mixtures of coloured stone and brick demonstrates the extent of Ruskin's influence. Almost every kind of building could be made to take on a Lombardic or Venetian look. With varying degrees of restraint houses, terraces, schools, town halls, court houses and railway stations developed coloured stripes and pointed windows decorated with naturalistic foliage carved in stone. The style was particularly popular for churches which gave opportunities for arcades with marble columns and towers like campaniles. Some of the most vigorous examples occurred in Belfast where the manner was widely accepted for warehouses and public buildings. Among these the most scholarly and the most full blooded are the designs by William Henry Lynn (1829-1915) who is exceptional among Ulster architects for the ease with which he manages the full vocabulary of Ruskinian Gothic features in a wide variety of coherent designs. Nowhere is this more apparent than at the Church of Ireland Offices, May Street (1867), with its brilliant decorative brickwork and stone carving; there is even a balcony over the front door so that pale maidens may acknowledge the love songs of passing gondoliers. Lynn's work in a similar vein may be admired at the Water Office, Donegall Square (1869), and the Old Library, Queen's University (1865 and 1912).

RUSKINIAN GOTHIC

Left: *Belfast (Northern) Bank, Newtownards Co. Down (Lanyon & Lynn 1854)*

Railway Building

The spread of the railway system across Ulster occurred during the middle years of the 19th Century and the building associated with the lines, stations, bridges, viaducts, engine sheds and stores, reflects the current architectural trends. The earliest stations like that remaining at Moira (1841) and that now gone in Great Victoria Street, Belfast (1846) were dressed in early Victorian stucco with heavily moulded arched windows and strong cornices. Later stations show architectural fashions adopted by various railway companies: Gothic at Newtownbutler and Lisbellaw (1858); polychrome brick at Lisburn (1878) and Cookstown (1879); Italianate at Coleraine (1855) and Derry Waterside (1873). More individual is the Scottish baronial station

Below: *Moira Station, Co. Antrim (1841)*

RAILWAY BUILDING

built for Lord Dufferin at Helen's Bay (c1865), which combines pointed, lancet windows with moulded arches and crow-step gables. At the end of the century the arts-and-crafts fashion resulted in the dramatic 'Elizabethan' timbered station at Portrush (1892). Nor were the other buildings associated with the railways less distinguished; viaducts, in particular, like those at Dromore, Co. Down, and Randalstown, Co. Antrim, are among the province's most impressive structures; and even these look relatively insignificant in relation to the awesome Craigmore-Mullaghglass viaduct which carries the Belfast-Dublin railway in a great curve over its eighteen arches, each spanning 60 feet, and reaches 150 feet above ground level.

Above: *Helen's Bay Railway Station, Co. Down (Benjamin Ferrey c1865)*

THE NINETEENTH CENTURY

Left: *St. Patrick's Roman Catholic Cathedral, Armagh (1840-1873)*

GOTHIC REVIVAL

The revival of serious Gothic architecture gathered momentum during the 1840s encouraged by the deliberations of such societies as the Down and Connor Church Architecture Society, founded in 1843. With its close ties with England and its secure financial position, the Church of Ireland inevitably took the lead, though the influence of Augustus Pugin, the principal English revivalist, who had become a Roman Catholic, was perhaps understandably ultimately strongest in the building of Roman Catholic churches. The progress of the Gothic Revival may be concisely illustrated by the development of St. Patrick's R.C. Cathedral, Armagh. Thomas Duff's original design begun in 1840 was in the late Gothic style which had already achieved popular success at St. Patrick and Colman's, Newry and St. Patrick's Dundalk. His are the doorways with square-headed mouldings and the elaborately decorated lower windows. Work was brought to a halt in 1846 because of the famine and Duff died two

GOTHIC REVIVAL

years later. It was not until 1854 that the building was recommenced and by that time there was a demand for the earlier, more simple Gothic style. The cathedral was completed by James McCarthy whose redrawn design laid emphasis on the west front with its twin towers, simple belfry openings and soaring spires. McCarthy, the most important Dublin architect of his generation, who became known as the 'Irish Pugin', designed many of his best churches for Ulster including cathedrals at Monaghan, Derry and Letterkenny, and churches at Cookstown and Dungannon.

It was Thomas Duff's early partner, Thomas Jackson, who, soon after the two decided to have separate practices, designed St Malachy's Roman Catholic Church, Alfred Street, Belfast (1840-1844). The church has a traditional T-shape but it is very large and in a full-blooded Tudor Revival style. The exterior has a variety of late Gothic windows on two levels, clasping buttresses, crenellated parapets, and two turrets at the end of each part of the 'T' with a larger bell turret over the joint of the 'T'. But it is the inside which has the great surprise. Tall windows light the gallery and above the whole ceiling is covered with decorative plasterwork arranged as tangent circles with pendent vaults like those in Henry VII's Chapel at Westminster.

Below: *Newry Cathedral, Co. Down*

Above: *St. Patrick's Church, Jordanstown, County Antrim (1866)*

CELTIC REVIVAL

While the Roman Catholic churches maintained a predominantly Gothic character, those of the Church of Ireland showed a wider range of origins. Gothic was the rule in the 1850s but after 1860 the influence of Ruskin became apparent in the mixing of coloured stone and brick, and a more adventurous approach to the arrangement of plans. Perhaps in some forlorn attempt to maintain its privileged position as the Established Church, particular attention was paid to Ireland's own medieval churches; the result was the Celtic Revival. St. Patrick's Parish Church, Jordanstown, (1866) was the first to revive the Celtic style in a whole-hearted and scholarly way. It was designed by W.H. Lynn who had had the advantage two years before of rebuilding the real medieval church of St. Doulough, Co. Dublin. St. Patrick's has the tall, sharply pointed gables and deep, round arches of Hiberno-Romanesque buildings such as Cormac's Chapel, Cashel

CELTIC REVIVAL

Below: *St Matthew's Church, Woodvale Road, Belfast (1870-2, Welland & Gillespie)*

Above: *St. Patrick's Church, Ballyclog, Co Tyrone (1865)*

(1127-34), while the layout of the church with the round tower joining the south side of the chancel derives from Temple Finghin at Clonmacnoise, Co. Offaly. Less scholarly but more original were the works of Welland & Gillespie, architects to the Ecclesiastical Commissioners. St Patrick's, Ballyclog, Co.Tyrone (1865) is a small country church which blends Irish elements – steep roof and round tower - with polychromatic construction to very original effect. St. Matthew's, Woodvale Road, Belfast, (1870) is an extrovert polychrome brick composition with a round tower and a quatrefoil plan (which is commonly believed to have been intended to suggest the shape of a shamrock). Later in the century the style became popular for Catholic churches such as that at Raphoe, Co. Donegal (Timothy Hevey, 1874).

THE NINETEENTH CENTURY

HIGH VICTORIAN MONUMENTS

Among the most expressive examples of the mixed, High Victorian style are the memorial clock towers and fountains which often form the focus for street junctions. The largest and perhaps the most successful is the Albert Memorial Clock Tower at the foot of the High Street, Belfast. Taking its main form from that of an Italian campanile, it has north European features as well, such as heraldic lions with shields and flying buttresses. Smaller but equally good in detail is the sadly neglected Martin Memorial at Shrigley, Co Down with marble columns, polychrome stone and intricate ironwork. The Rossmore Memorial, centrepiece of the Diamond, Monaghan, is a more slender but similar design.

Above and right: *Albert Memorial, High Street, Belfast (1865 W.J. Barre)*

HIGH VICTORIAN MONUMENTS

Right: *Martin Memorial, Shrigley, County Down (1370 Timothy Hevey)*

THE NINETEENTH CENTURY

VICTORIAN COMMERCIAL

The progress of Ulster's architecture in the second half of the 19th Century is seen in the developing style and scale of its commercial buildings. Ruskin's polychrome mixture was replaced by an elaborate classicism. Belfast, the centre of increasing prosperity, began to afford large quantities of imported stone, a material hitherto reserved largely for the town's churches. Better stone made the design of sculptural façades more adventurous. The splendid façade of Lytle's and McCausland's, Victoria Street (1866-7) is actually carved partly as advertisement for their seed businesses. Lytle's façade has carved capitals alive with creatures happily munching (seeds?) among the vegetation. McCausland, with wider horizons, has pilasters carved as figureheads representing the five continents and festoons of their fruit.

There is also a gradual increase in scale. Ewart's fine building barely exceeds the three-storey scale of the Georgian town; twenty years later Robinson and Cleaver's store is double the height and making an even more dramatic use of its advantageous corner site at Donegall Square.

Left: *Ewart's, Bedford Street, Belfast (1869 James Hamilton)*

VICTORIAN COMMERCIAL

Above: *McCausland's (1866-7 William Hastings)*

THE NINETEENTH CENTURY

VICTORIAN PUBLIC BUILDINGS

Victorian public buildings play an important part in Ulster's townscapes, dominating junctions and vistas. Victorian architects became particularly adept at arranging elements of a building within its ground plan so as to give maximum effect to a variety of views. Downpatrick Assembly Rooms (William Batt, architect, 1878) was designed as more than a social centre for the town; it is also an architectural focus. Its tower placed at the corner of the building can be seen along the converging streets. Closer views show that the façade is designed to distinguish between the use of the various parts of the building. The irregularity of the openings on the ground floor corresponds intentionally with its varied functions as office, shop and entrance hall. Up above, the grand evenly placed windows belong, as they would in a real Venetian palace of the type which this imitates, to the principal rooms. In a more formal way Enniskillen Town Hall (William Scott, architect, 1899) dominates the Diamond and the main street, while its cupola-topped tower balances the cathedral spire on the crest of the island's other hill. It has the large-scale, rather pompous Classical façades so much admired at the end of Victoria's reign.

Left: *Assembly Rooms, Downpatrick, County Down (1878, William Batt)*

VICTORIAN PUBLIC BUILDINGS

Right: *Town Hall, Enniskillen, County Fermanagh (1899, William Scott)*

Victorian Entertainment

Some late Victorian buildings are so elaborate externally as to appear ostentatious and vulgar. But such excesses indoors can produce opulent richness and enjoyable gaiety. This was no doubt the intention of those who designed the great palaces of Victorian entertainment, the theatres, opera houses and music halls. Frank Matcham (c1855-1920), a London architect, was the most experienced theatre specialist of his generation. His Grand Opera House, Great Victoria Street, Belfast (1894) is the last surviving old-style theatre in Ulster and its interior decoration ranks with some of the best in Britain. The exterior which has suffered some remodelling is interesting rather than exciting. A wing was added to one side in contemporary style in 2006. Inside, however, there is an atmosphere of exotic abandon. Decoration is lavished everywhere, from the panelled columns of the pit to the plaster framework of the ceiling paintings. Balcony fronts, heavy with vegetable relief and oriental goddesses, sway between columns mounted with elephants' heads. Layers of boxes with gilt frames and velvet hangings rise to roofs with onion domes.

The famous Victorian gin-palace, the Crown Bar, also lies on Great Victoria Street. It was remodelled internally in 1885 and externally in 1895 by E and J. Byrne, architects. Like the stables of a fabulous Oriental potentate, its snugs are ranged along the walls, like loose boxes, set amidst a profusion of mosaic floors, coloured glass, mirrors and decorated ceilings.

Left: *Interior of the Grand Opera House, Great Victoria Street, Belfast (1894)*

VICTORIAN ENTERTAINMENT

Below: *The Crown Bar, Belfast*

Above: *City Hall, Donegall Square, Belfast (1896-1906, A. Brumwell Thomas)*

LATE VICTORIAN PUBLIC BUILDING

Belfast's emerging identity at the turn of the century as the capital of the industrial north is nowhere better illustrated in architectural terms than in the building of the City Hall, which replaced the old White Linen Hall (1785) in Donegall Square. Belfast had achieved the status of a city in 1888 less than twenty years after the completion of the Town Hall in Victoria Street. It is indicative of the confident spirit prevailing at the time that such an ambitious undertaking should have been projected so soon; yet the building accurately reflects that spirit with its assured presence. Many parts of the building have been directly borrowed. Sir Brumwell Thomas, the architect, came from London so it is no surprise to find London buildings by Gibbs and Nash being used. The thinly disguised adaptation of the dome and corner towers from Wren's St. Paul's Cathedral is slightly more startling. Yet these details are of little individual importance, for it is the design as a whole (which the recent cleaning has greatly emphasised) which gives the building its satisfying poise.

LATE VICTORIAN PUBLIC BUILDING

Right: *City Hall, Donegall Square, Belfast (1896-1906) interior view*

THE NINETEENTH CENTURY

Right: *Robinson & Cleaver Building, Donegall Square North (1886-88, Young & Mackenzie)*

LATE VICTORIAN COMMERCIAL

The spirit of confidence which brought about the erection of the City Hall can be paralleled in contemporary private projects, especially among those which were built as the City Hall's immediate neighbours. The building of Anderson and McAuley's store (1895) and the Scottish Provident Institution (1897-1902), both by Young and Mackenzie, architects, also span the turn of the century. On a site which gave less scope for dramatic sculptural display, the latter building contrives, from the front at least, to be both grand and interesting. In the manner typical of the Late Victorian period a style, Palladian in this case, has been taken and inflated. Thus the rusticated basement on which the columns rest is two storeys high while the columns themselves rise through three further storeys. An elaborate, pedimented attic and octagonal corner pavilions with domes enliven the skyline. Perhaps the most unusual feature of the building is the bulging centre with coupled columns, which seems to have less in common with proper rounded bows than with the nervous curving of Art Nouveau (see p. 178).

LATE VICTORIAN COMMERCIAL

Left: *Scottish Provident Institution, Donegall Square West, Belfast (1897-1902, Young & Mackenzie). Corner Cupola*

Overleaf: *Scottish Provident Institution, Donegall Square West, Belfast (1897-1902).*

SCOTTISH PROVID
Hoggs
The Gift House of Ulst
Clarkes of donegall sq.
PHOTOGRAPHY
COVERS

Miselle   The Shirt Centre

The Twentieth Century

THE TWENTIETH CENTURY

Previous page: *Window, Castle Buildings, Castle Place, Belfast. (1905-5)*

M. Crymble Ltd (Former), Music Depot, Wellington Place, Belfast (W.J. Roome, 1903)

ART NOUVEAU DECORATION

The decoration of buildings in the Edwardian period was not merely, not even generally, an extension of the overblown classicism of late Victoriana. Many new influences began to emerge and of these the most immediate and the most distinctive was the tide of Art Nouveau which had begun as a wayward decorative manner of great originality in Belgium. Among the many Ulster architects who were influenced was W. J. W. Roome, whose design of 1903 for the front of Crymble's music shop in Wellington Place, Belfast, combines a range of typically novel features with curving lines, cheerful colour and clear lettering. The shop is still there, and in good order, but, because it is no longer Crymble's, and the letters have been painted out, the effect is less striking. Another example close-by, at 36, Donegall Place, Belfast, is the former building of Sharman D. Neill, designed by Vincent Craig in 1903. Here the three upper floors have a splendid collection of historic details wrapped about with typical, Art Nouveau 'melting' curves. Again, unfortunately, the full effect was compromised many years ago when the contrasting brick and sandstone was all painted one colour. A similar very free assembly of historical details is to be found on the surviving upper parts of the artificial stone front of the Castle Buildings, in Castle Place, Belfast, designed from 1904 by Percy Morgan Jury of Blackwood and Jury. Perhaps the most original and distinctive feature of Art Nouveau design, the 'whiplash curve' is used in the relief decoration and balcony ironwork.

ART NOUVEAU DECORATION

Right: *Castle Buildings, Castle Place, Belfast. (Blackwood and Jury, 1904-5)*

The Twentieth Century

Art Nouveau Churches

The Art Nouveau style is also to be found in more rural settings in Ulster, including a number of churches, where its effects tend to be confined to Non-Conformist works. One exponent of the style was Blackwood and Jury, whose Trinity Presbyterian Church in Letterkenny is an example of their work (1907). Vincent Craig's Hill Hall Presbyterian Church is perhaps the best Ulster church to use this style of architecture. It was built in 1901-1902 and is a large T-shaped building, with roughcast walls, Bath stone trim and an entrance porch at the base of the tower. The pattern of alternating chequers in the gable's tympanum is characteristic of the kind of originality which architects working in this style strove to achieve. Unusual and surprising shapes

Below: *Hill Hall Presbyterian Church, Co. Down (1901)*

or improbable construction details were often a feature; indeed, the style even extends to the design of the gate posts. In a similar if rather more restrained manner Vincent Craig produced designs for Presbyterian churches at Portstewart (1902) and Ballywatt, near Portrush (1910-11).

Below left: *Presbyterian Church, Ballywatt, Co. Antrim (1910-11)*

Below right: *Presbyterian Church, Portstewart, Co. Londonderry (1902)*

THE TWENTIETH CENTURY

Above: *Bank Buildings, Castle Place, Belfast (1900, W.H. Lynn)*

EDWARDIAN COMMERCIAL BUILDINGS

Most of Belfast's really grand commercial designs had been built by the end of the 19th Century, but the Edwardian era saw a number of notable additions, for example the Ocean Building (Young and Mackenzie 1902) and the Scottish Mutual Building (Seaver, 1904), on Donegall Square, and the Bank Building in Castle Place (W.H. Lynn, 1900). The Bank Building, constructed with cast iron piers inside, is composed of Dumfries red sandstone and massive Corinthian columns in polished granite.

Outside Belfast there were less opportunities for such imposing buildings. The best of the large Edwardian stores is undoubtably Austin's in the Diamond at Londonderry, designed by M.A. Robinson in 1906. Here are combined all that was good about late Victorian streetscaping and all that was exciting and inventive in Edwardian decoration. A six-storey tower with fish-scale dome and spike surmounts the corner while to each side attached columns attempt to restore some calm to façades piled with irregularly curved windows. The windows of the mansard roof are particularly effective with highly ornate flowing decoration. Because historic details from a wide range of sources were adapted, exaggerated, mixed or used in inappropriate positions – and all for the sake of the whole effect – the style has become known as Edwardian 'Freestyle'.

EDWARDIAN COMMERCIAL BUILDINGS

Right: *Austin and Co. Ltd, the Diamond, Londonderry (1906, M.A. Robinson)*

THE TWENTIETH CENTURY

ARTS AND CRAFTS HOUSES

Art Nouveau decoration was only one rather colourful facet of a wide revolt against the boredom of 19th Century revivalism coupled with a demand for a new style. The Modern Movement, as this attitude is now designated, has several origins. The desire for simplicity and buildings uncluttered with historical features derives from William Morris's Arts and Crafts influence in the mid-19th Century. Morris abhorred the mass productions of the machine age and attempted in vain to return to the irregular but more agreeable qualities of handicraft. Simplicity of decoration and functional planning were the very essence of such houses, a good example being 'Dallas' on the Malone Road, Belfast, built in 1911 by Charles F. Annesley Voysey, the most important follower of Morris. In Ulster the Arts and Crafts movement was boosted by imports such as the half-timbered Sion House, Sion Mills, Co. Tyrone, built in 1883 for the Herdman family by an English relative, William Unsworth, architect of the original Shakespeare Memorial Theatre at Stratford-on-Avon. Among the first local architects to develop the style was William Scott at Killyhevlin House, Enniskillen, Co. Fermanagh (1903), and Cavan Town Hall (1908-10). The most concentrated development of the style, however, was in and around Belfast which, expanding and wealthy, had achieved city status in 1888. One of its prosperous merchants, Ernest Herdman, in 1906-08 built Glenmakieran House in Hollywood, Co Down in the 'free-style'. It is

Right: *Sion House, Sion Mills, Co. Tyrone (post 1883, Unsworth)*

ARTS AND CRAFTS HOUSES

Left: *'Dallas', Malone Road, Belfast (1911, Voysey)*

notable for its Lutyens's style windows, tall clustered chimney-stacks and steep red-tile roofs. There are many good suburban examples in Belfast's upper Malone area, but few are as full-blooded, both outside and inside, as Haslemere, 46, Myrtlefield Park, Belfast designed for himself in 1905 by Frederick Tulloch of Watt, Tulloch and Fitzsimons. The only Ulster design by Sir Edwin Lutyens, the outstanding Arts and Crafts and Classical designer in England, was a holiday house, now Tranarossan Youth Hostel, Co. Donegal. His is a celebration of the mason's craft – a pair of linked blocks with granite walls and piers, a roof of huge slates and slate hung gables.

Left: *Glenmakieran, Co. Down (1906, Unsworth)*

OFFICIAL (CLASSICAL) BUILDINGS

While the Modern Movement was being pursued abroad, the public buildings of Ulster, like those of the rest of Britain and Ireland, settled down to a rather sterile, official classicism. Often this was stereotyped and dull but the more imaginative architects could produce buildings with dignity and originality and even on occasion features that manage to introduce rather unexpected whimsy and amusement. Only one wing of the Ulster (originally Belfast Municipal) Museum, as designed by J.C. Wynnes in 1911, was built. Even so its façades are hardly uneventful. Above a very heavily rusticated ground floor, the upper floors are also rusticated though with finer channelling. The corners are emphasised with projections set away from the corner which have Ionic columns set in antis (into the front of the wall) and attics which have inwards curves apparently designed to shelter urns from the wind. At one place the façade is interrupted by the stone-carved figurehead and prow of a clinker-built ship. This high unorthodox departure from strict classicism was no doubt considered earnestly appropriate for ship-building Belfast. When, eventually, the museum was extended (1963-71) to something like its original intended size, the architect, Francis Pym, extended some of the features of the older part of the building, through into the thoroughly modern concrete portion. The result was a successful blend of two different traditions into a single dramatic composition.

Left: *Ulster Museum, Stranmillis Road, Belfast (1911-1920)*

OFFICIAL (CLASSICAL) BUILDINGS

Left: *Bank of Ireland, Conway Square, Newtownards, Co. Down (c1915-1920)*

A smaller instance of rather mannered handling of Classical features is the Bank of Ireland in Conway Square, Newtownards (c1915-1920) where, in a very un-classical way, a single column and two halves add a touch of eccentricity to an otherwise dignified façade.

Neo-Georgian Buildings

Turning from the Gothic Revival, Ulster architects followed those in Britain in avoiding modern trends and developing instead the style which has become known as Neo-Georgian. They returned to the features which had fallen into disrepute during the Victorian period. Classical doorways with fanlights or columns took their place once more in the centre of façades. Regular bays of windows glazed with small panes introduced a new serenity after the haphazard arrangement of Arts and Crafts elevations (see p.184). Official architects used the style with much success. In 1929 R. Ingleby Smith (Chief Architect) and T.F.O. Rippingham (Principal Designer) designed Stranmillis College for the Ministry of Finance - a building which responds to the advantages of its spacious site with axial grandeur. The centre of the façade with its modestly scaled front door is emphasised by the surmounting temple lantern. To left and right advancing wings are joined to the main block by curving bays with elaborate doorways and recessed columns. The mansard roof of pantiles with corniced dormers, in combination with the red brick walls, gives the college a pleasant French flavour.

The Neo-Georgian style could also be used in a less demonstrative manner, more in keeping with the naturally reticent tone of Ulster building

Below: *Stranmillis College, Belfast (1929, Smith and Rippingham)*

NEO-GEORGIAN BUILDINGS

in general. This is most outstanding in the series of Royal Ulster Constabulary stations which were built in the decade following partition. Their basic design, the work of T.F.O. Rippingham, while having its own distinct identity derived some of its elements from earlier types of building in the province. The combination of hipped roof with chimneys rising from the end walls looks back to the early 18th Century (p.82), while the arched recesses of the front door and its flanking windows borrowed from the Regency or Late Georgian styles (p.128) give the façade a simple yet positive dignity. The design was adaptable in size varying from three windows in width to eight or nine; it also proved an environmental success, blending with the older buildings along the streets of Ulster's towns, or taking its place quietly in more isolated country situations. As an instance of official design respecting the character of the province, it set an example which its successors have all too frequently failed to follow.

The arrival of these first essays in the modern style coincided with the design of the two latest, largest and most impressive of Ulster's official Classical buildings. The Royal Courts of Justice in Chichester Street, Belfast (J.G. West, 1928-33) demonstrates with grand façades of giant columns and ornate window frames the lasting popularity of the early 18th Century style of James Gibbs. By contrast with the frenzy of Art Deco, the Parliament Buildings at Stormont, built in 1927-33 to designs of the Liverpool architect Arnold Thornley, have a sombre and dignified strength. The design derived ultimately from that of a Palladian house with the portico raised on a rusticated ground floor and the principal decoration concentrated about the first floor windows. Above the sculptured pediment rises a lavishly

Above: *Former Police Station, Seaforde, County Down (1930, Thomas F.O. Rippingham)*

THE TWENTIETH CENTURY

Above: *The Government Buildings, Stormont, County Down (1927-33, A. Thornley)*

decorated attic surmounted by the figure of Britannia flanked by lions. The impact of the composition is much enhanced by the staggeringly bold treatment of the landscape (laid out by H. Armytage Moore). From the heroic main gates on the Dundonald Road a straight drive, approaching a mile in length, mounts directly to the great flights of steps in front of the main portico. In this progress it is punctuated only once, where crossdrives converge on the Leninesque statue of Carson. Equally impressive is the progress from beneath the portico to the central marble hall with as its focus at the far end a bronze statue of Lord Craigavon raised on the central half-landing of the great staircase.

Above: *Royal Courts of Justice, Chichester Street, Belfast (1928-33)*

Art Deco

While the official architects of the province were content to do without the modern style, and while local architects in general seemed unattracted by it, it was nevertheless to be thrust upon them. The Bank of Ireland, Royal Avenue, Belfast, built in 1928-9, has the honour of being the first building in Ulster to introduce the modern style which the Paris Exposition of 1925 had made popular in Europe. The Bank was designed by McConnell, Dixon and Downes, who in their Dublin practice were closer to the influence of such novel buildings as the Church of Christ the King at Cork, designed in 1925 by Barry Byrne of Chicago. The Bank of Ireland in Belfast was not generally admired; its style was even referred to as 'fascist' and indeed it is not far removed in some details from the architecture of Mussolini. The windows are bound together into tall strips and the decoration reduced to series of blocky vertical slices. It was not long, however, before the details of the bank, if not its total spirit, were being adopted. Across the road is Sinclair's store (J. Scott, 1935) another fine block in this modern style with the pyramidal front which was to become the hallmark of generations of cinemas and garages (noticeably those types of building for which the modern manner was considered appropriate). The style known simply as 'modern' at the time of its arrival has since been termed 'Art-Deco' or in one of the more appropriate comparisons between music and architecture as 'Jazz Age Modern'.

Left: *Bank of Ireland, Royal Avenue, Belfast (1928, McConnell, Dixon & Downes)*

ART DECO

Above: *Sinclair's store, Royal Avenue, Belfast (1935, J. Scott)*

Left: *Somerset's Linen Factory*
(1904, W.J.W. Roome)

Concrete Framed Buildings

With Ulster's strong engineering tradition and shipbuilding reputation it was perhaps natural that her architects should take a lively interest in technical advances in architectural construction. The system of ferro-concrete construction devised by the French engineer, François Hennebique was patented by him in 1892. It involved using structural beams of concrete reinforced with stirrups and longitudinal bars designed to resist considerable tensile forces. Hennebique's system was used as early as 1904 by the architect W. J. W. Roome on the former Somerset Linen factory in Hardcastle Street, Belfast. Hennebique's British representative Louis Mouchel was involved here in the specialist ferro-concrete work, while a seven storey extension by Blackwood and Jury in 1911 also used the same system. Outside of Belfast concrete reinforced with a core of steel rods had been used by William Scott for the dome of his convent chapel at Enniskillen in 1904. The same architect's hostel at St. Patrick's Purgatory, Lough Derg, Co. Donegal (1910-12) also employed a skeletal frame of steel and concrete.

The Hennebique system was also used on bridges. An early example is one at Corratory, on a remote mountain road between Draperstown and Plumbridge built in 1920. Two early triple-span reinforced concrete bridges were built at Inishkerragh and Portinode in 1925-7, linking Boa Island to the mainland. These allowed travellers to drive between Kesh and Belleek by avoiding border customs post at Pettigoe.

CONCRETE FRAMED BUILDINGS

Above: *Portinode Bridge, Boa Island. Co. Fermanagh (1925-7, J. Burkitt)*

Left: *Corratary Bridge, Corramore Road, Co. Tyrone (1920, C.L. Boddie)*

THE TWENTIETH CENTURY

Below: *Enniskillen Masonic Hall, Co. Fermanagh (1930-31)*

MODERNISTIC FUNCTIONAL

The introduction of modernistic decoration was often accompanied by the use of new building techniques. The full potential of concrete was brought to a wider audience in Ulster with the opening of the King's Hall at Balmoral, Belfast (Leitch and Partners, Glasgow, 1933). The pyramidal façade with Art Deco motifs on the doors and buttresses (and gates and gateposts) shields a highly functional space spanned by reinforced concrete arches and lit by stepped clerestory windows. Significantly, like so many of the principal buildings of the period, it was designed by a firm from outside the province. In more conventional materials local architects were becoming modern. By degrees the Neo-Georgian style was replaced by a more original, blocky manner, using flat roofs, tall strips of window, and localised Art Deco carving. The Enniskillen Masonic

MODERNISTIC FUNCTIONAL

Left: *The Sir William Whitla Hall, Queen's University, Belfast (1938-49 Edward Maufe and John McGeagh)*

Overleaf: *The King's Hall, Lisburn Road, Balmoral, Belfast (1933-4 Leitch and Partners)*

Hall (1930-1) with its varied windows enlivening the red brick core and flanking, lower blocks, was a forerunner of the more ambitious Whitla Hall (1939-49), the first building to break with the Tudor Revival tradition of the Queen's University, Belfast. This was designed in 1937 by John MacGeagh with consulting architect Edward Maufe, but not completed until after the war in 1949. Equally notable are the school designs by R.S. Wilshere such as the Elmgrove (1932) and Botanic Primary (1936) Schools, Belfast.

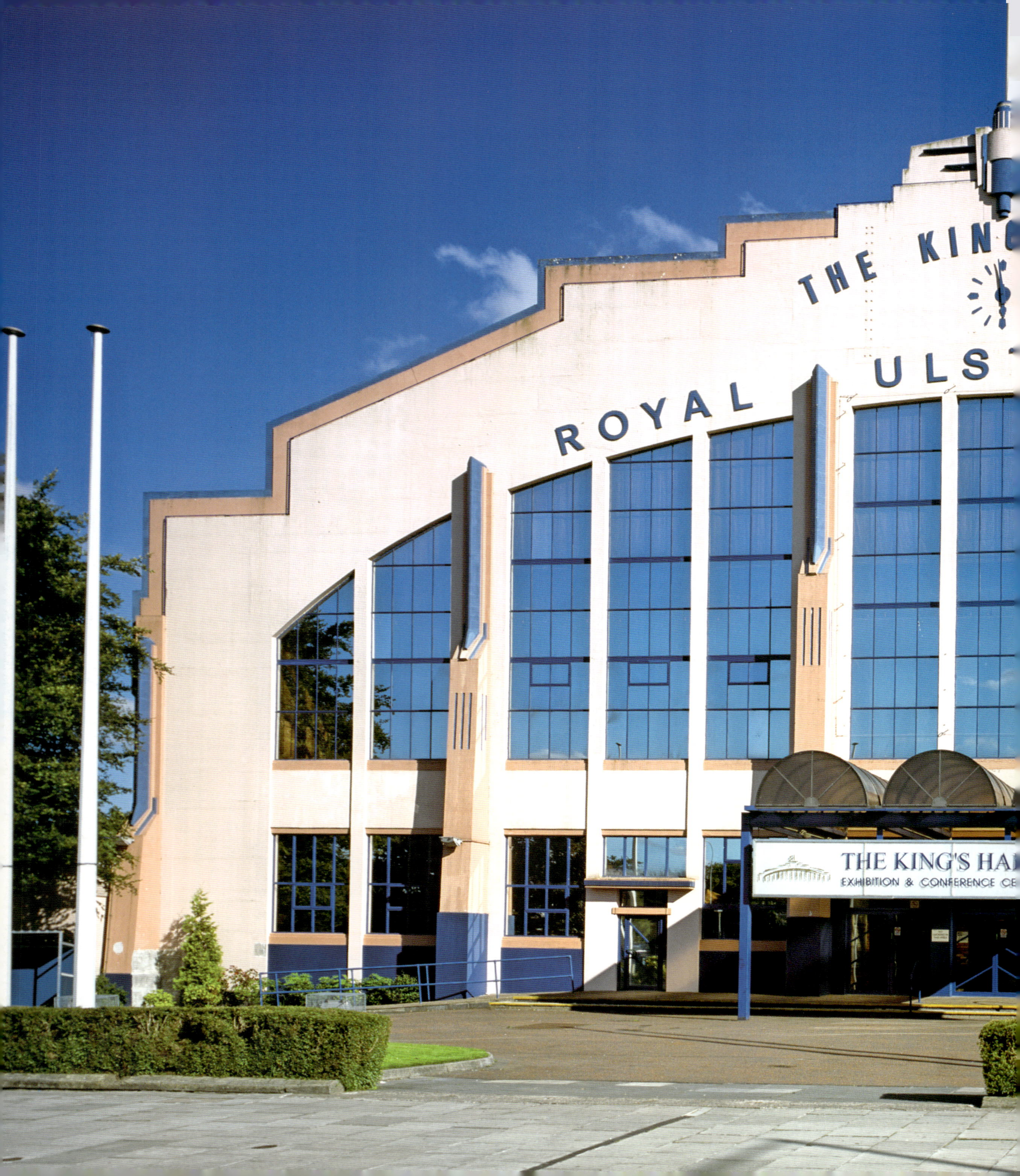
THE KING
ROYAL ULS
THE KING'S HA
EXHIBITION & CONFERENCE CE

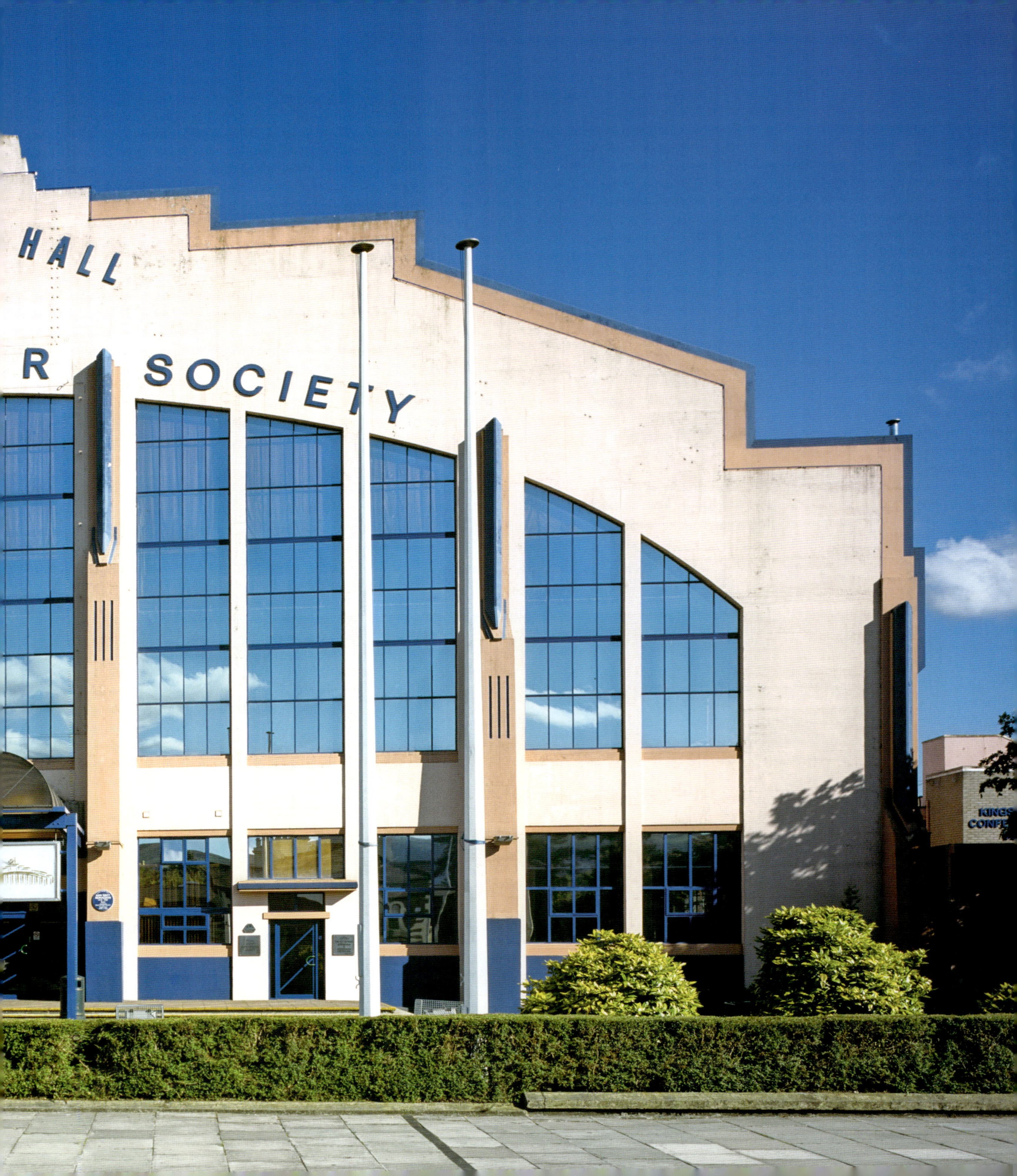
HALL
R SOCIETY

Twentieth Century Housing

Late Victorian historicism and the Arts-and-Crafts movement dominated domestic design until the Great War. Between the wars there was surprisingly little housebuilding though the first modern designs from a local office were produced in 1934 by G.P. Bell at Moyallen, Co. Armagh. The flat roof, hallmark of the new style, had appeared (to the amazement of the architectural press) on Belfast houses as early as 1895, and was used for such large buildings as the Mater Hospital (W.J. Fennell, 1900). It was not to achieve general popularity, however, until after the Second World War. Alexander Crescent, Armagh, is a typical, suburban council development of the post-war period. The semi-detached houses have a rather boxy appearance and such modernistic details as angled front doors flanked by strips of glass brick. In retrospect the wide use of pre-fabricated houses may be regarded with greater favour than subsequent experiments with high-rise blocks, though the limitations of each are severe. Recent public housing projects have shown a welcome trend towards greater sympathy with the character of local architecture. In some cases old buildings are themselves being restored (Alexander Memorial Cottages, Londonderry). Elsewhere new houses are designed to blend with

Below: *Alexander Crescent, Armagh (G.P. Bell For Armagh U.D.C.1948-50)*

TWENTIETH CENTURY HOUSING

Above: *Shore Cottages, Portaferry, County Down (1973, McAdam Design Partnership for Northern Ireland Housing Executive)*

existing ones (Tandragee, Purdysburn Village, Co. Down). The rebuilding of the Shore Cottages at Portaferry has been particularly successful, providing up-to-date accommodation while retaining the character and informality of one of Ulster's most important townscapes.

INTERNATIONAL STYLE

Functional architecture derives more or less from the belief that if a building works well, then it is beautiful. Its development was encouraged early in the century in France by the visions of Tony Garnier and the concrete of Le Corbusier, in America by the skyscrapers of Louis Sullivan and the moody genius of his pupil, Frank Lloyd Wright, and in Germany by the example at the Bauhaus of Walter Gropius and Mies van der Rohe. The result was simple blocks of unadorned building boldly displaying their method of construction; they occur all over the world and as a result the style has become known as International. It dominated Ulster architecture during the 1950s and 1960s, most especially the design of large buildings, factories, hospitals, of-

Ulster College of Art, York Street, Belfast (1969-70) Original design by Donald Shanks for Education Department: executed by J.H. Swann, City Architect.

INTERNATIONAL STYLE

fice and housing blocks. The Ulster College of Art (the province's own Bauhaus) discloses its structure through glass curtain walls. The lines of the design are clean but the façades have the flat impersonality typical of the period. Elsewhere attempts were made to counteract the severe lack of decoration; the Altnagelvin Hospital, Londonderry, (Yorke, Rosenberg and Mardell, 1949-59) received sculpture; Dundonald House, Co. Down (Gibson and Taylor, 1963) was given a curve; the Ashby Institute, Queen's University, Belfast (Cruickshank and Seward, 1964) gained a wafer-patterned strip of white concrete. Soon the demand for purely functional design diminished and more radical methods were sought to endow buildings with some of their former interest.

Ashby Institute, Belfast
(1960-5, Cruickshank & Seward)

Above: *Music Department, Stranmillis College, Belfast (1970)*

CONCRETE & BRICK SCULPTURAL

In their attempt to dispel the boredom of the International Style architects looked increasingly to the strength and versatility of reinforced concrete. Hitherto the use of this method of construction had been largely restricted to the building of regular frames; now its sculptural possibilities began to be realised. Reaching out from the quadrangle of the Central Building at Stranmillis College, the Music Department takes advantage of the sloping site to sprout like a mushroom; the effect is decisive and agreeable. Concrete rarely looks attractive and here it is concealed behind applied panels of mosaic pebbles. Between these, windows like facets catch the light and give the whole building a lively extra dimension. Concrete can be used in a more direct way. The enlargement of the Ulster Museum (Francis Pym, 1971) was achieved with much success by extending some of the Classical features of the original building to melt gradually into a boldly sculptural, concrete composition 'like a dresser with the drawers left open'. The chief setback of such schemes has been the unsightly discolouring of the concrete, a problem shared by many of the province's civil engineering structures. As Ulster's most ambitious building ventures, motorways, roads, dams and bridges should be designed with regard for both stability and visual sensitivity. An outstanding example of such a blend is the M2 Motorway intersection at Greencastle, County Antrim, where parallel bridges in-

CONCRETE & BRICK SCULPTURAL

Ulster Museum extension, Belfast (1963-71, Francis Pym)

County Hall, Galgorm, Co. Antrim (1970) Burman and Goodall

cline, camber and curve all at once.

Sculptural effects can also be achieved using traditional materials. Brick continues to be used widely both for load-bearing and as a cladding material. The Antrim County Hall at Galgorm, completed in 1970, is a composition which gains immeasurably from its mantle of warm, brown bricks. The exterior of the Council Chamber in particular makes adventurous use of fragmented brickwalling about a fragmented pyramid. Such romantic originality is the hallmark of architectural developments in the 1970s.

205

St. Columba's Church of Ireland Church, Portadown, Co Armagh (1970, Gordon McKnight)

SYMBOLICAL SCULPTURAL

Symbolic shapes can also give buildings individual character. This is particularly the case with Ulster churches, which, because they had rarely been elaborate, could adapt their traditional design to the new material and functional structure of the International Style while avoiding its impersonality. The essence of the barn church (see p.76) was identified and revived by Denis O'D. Hanna in the 1950s and subsequently used by others. The timber portal frame of the Seymour Hill Presbyterian Church, Dunmurry, Co. Antrim (Munce and Kennedy, 1959) has gables high enough to give a modern echo to the Celtic style (p.160). The most enduring symbol, however, is the cruciform plan for churches. Its use for the crisply detailed St. Columba's Church, Portadown, unites modern building techniques with traditional forms; and the inclusion of a single stone from the ancient church of St. Columba, at Gartan, County Donegal emphasises a continuing heritage.

SYMBOLICAL SCULPTURAL

Right: *Seymour Hill Presbyterian Church, Dunmurry (1959, Munce and Kennedy)*

New Victoria College, Belfast (1968-72, Shanks & Leighton)

TOPOGRAPHICAL SCULPTURAL

An important development in the second half of the 20th Century has resulted from the careful attention paid by designers to the character of the province's landscape and townscape. Perhaps the most damaging aspect of post-war architecture was that, in its pursuit of the functional, it tended to disregard the traditions of local building, its materials, its style, above all its situation. An increasing awareness of Ulster's natural beauty, its architectural heritage, and how these affect one another, has led to a new and refreshingly sympathetic approach to the placing of buildings in both country and town. At Tandragee, Co. Armagh, terrace houses mould the old line of the main street and adopt the local variety of double-sash windows (N.I. Housing Executive, 1973). Victoria College, Belfast (Shanks and Leighton, 1972) melts unobtrusively into the wooded hillside of Cranmore Park. St. Michael's Church at Creeslough lifts a parabolic prow into the air to echo the distant line of Muckish mountain. This is the kind of care that architects can take; it is the kind of care that the subtle landscape of Ulster deserves.

TOPOGRAPHICAL SCULPTURAL

Above: *St. Michael's Roman Catholic Church, Creeslough, Co Donegal (1970-1, Liam McCormick and Partners)*

Right: *The Ferris Wheel, Donegall Square East, Belfast (2007)*

Bibliography

In 1975 a comprehensive bibliography relating to Ulster architecture covered just one admittedly rather crowded page. Now there is PADDI, the Planning Architecture Design Database for Ireland: www.paddi.net. This online database lists hundreds of works and collections relating to Ulster buildings. Perhaps there is no better indication of a change in attitude towards the province's building heritage than this – apart from the improved state of the buildings themselves.

This necessarily selective list has been divided into categories for convenience. Many of the books also contain their own bibliographies to which further reference may be made.

General Appreciations of Ulster Architecture

Brett, C.E.B. 1971. 'The architectural heritage' in *Causeway: the Arts in Ulster*. Dublin: Gill & Macmillan, pp.11-26

Boyd, B. 1986. *A Heritage from Stone: A Review of Architecture in Ulster from Prehistory to the Present Day*. Belfast: Ulster Television, 1986

Cornforth, John. 1984. 'Attitudes to Ulster towns. Conservation in Northern Ireland – I & II'. *Country Life*, CLXXVI (Nos. 4556-7), December 13th & 20th, pp1952-4.

Curl, James Stevens. 1981 'Ulster's traditional townscape'. *Country Life*, Vol. CLXIX (No. 4368), May 7th, pp1270

Evans, D. 1977. *An Introduction to Modern Ulster Architecture*. Belfast: UAHS. [sister volume to the 1975 edition of this *Introduction*, now superseded by Latimer, K. 2006 (see below)

Evans, D. & Patton, M. 1981. *The Diamond as Big as a Square*. Belfast: UAHS.

Hanna, D.O'D. 1951. 'Architecture in Ulster' in *The Arts in Ulster: A Symposium*. London: Harrap.

Jope, E.M. 1969. 'Introduction' in *Ancient Monuments of Northern Ireland: Vol. II: Not in State Care*. Belfast: HMSO.

Latimer, K. (ed.) 2006. *Modern Ulster Architecture*, UAHS. [David Evans and Paul Larmour provides an introduction to the province's building history post-1900; Charles Rattray sets the province in a wider context; Alastair Hall contributes to a series of case studies and Mark Hackett is responsible for most of the photography]

Oram, R. & Stelfox, J.D. 2004. *Traditional Buildings in Ireland: Home Owners Handbook*. Ireland: Mourne Heritage Trust.

Pierce, R., Coey, A and Oram, R. 1984. *Taken for Granted: A Celebration of 10 Years of Historic Building Conservation*. Northern Ireland: RSUA/Historic Buildings Council.

Rowan, A.J. 1971. 'Ulster's architectural identity'. *Country Life*, Vol. CXLIX (No. 3859), pp.1304-1306.

Works on particular aspects of Irish and Ulster Architecture

Aalen, F.H.A., Whelan, K & Stout, M. 1997. *Atlas of the Irish Rural Landscape*. Cork: Cork University Press. [includes chapters on building types, demesnes & industrial buildings]

Adams, C.L. 1904. *Castles of Ireland: Some Fortresses, Histories and Legends*. London: E. Stock. [a period piece from 'less stirring times'].

Bence-Jones, M. Burke's Guide to Country Houses 1978. Volume 1: Ireland London: Burke's Peerage Ltd. Revised edition, 1988, Constable.

Brett, C.E.B. 1973. *Court Houses and Market Houses of Ulster*. Belfast: UAHS.

Butler, D. M. 2004. *The Quaker Meeting Houses of Ireland*. Dublin: Irish Friends Historical Commission.

Caldwell, P. & Dixon, H. (eds) 1975. *Building Conservation in Northern Ireland*. DoENI. [a record of the campaign and projects for European Architectural Heritage Year]

Camblin, G. 1951. *The Town in Ulster*. Belfast: Mullan, 1951. [a history of planning in the province from the earliest times]

Champneys, A.C. 1910. *Irish Ecclesiastical Architecture*. Shannon: Irish University Press; reprinted 1970

Chart, D.A. (ed.) 1940. A *Preliminary Survey of the Ancient Monuments of Northern Ireland*. Belfast: HMSO.

Craig, M.J., and the Knight of Glin. 1965. *Irish Architectural Drawings*. Dublin: Municipal Gallery of Art illustrated catalogue, including drawings of some important Georgian buildings in Ulster; brief biographical notes..

Craig, M.J. 1976. *Classic Irish Houses of the Middle Size*. London: Architectural Press rep Ashfield Press, 2006.

BIBLIOGRAPHY

Cruickshank, D 1985. *A Guide to Georgian Buildings of Britain and Ireland.* London, Weidenfeld and Nicholson, the National Trust and the Irish Georgian Society

Curl, J.S. 1978. *Mausolea in Ulster.* Belfast: UAHS.

Curl, J.S. 1980. *Classical Churches in Ulster.* Belfast: UAHS.

Dean, J.A.K. 1994. *The Gate Lodges of Ulster.* Belfast: UAHS [a well illustrated gazetteer of gate lodges in the nine counties]

De Breffny, B. and Ffolliott, R. 1975. *The Houses of Ireland.* London: Thames & Hudson. [an excellently illustrated study including many Ulster houses]

Dixon, H. *Ulster Architecture 1800-1900.* 1972. Belfast: UAHS. [illustrated catalogue of 150 drawings, with biographical notes on architects]

Evans, E.E. 1957. *Irish Folk Ways.* London: Routledge. 5th impression 1972. [chapters on vernacular building]

Gaffikin, P. 1999. *Set in Stone: A Geological Guide to the Building Stones of Belfast.* Belfast: Environment & Heritage Service.

Gailey, A.. et al. 1974. *Rural Housing in Ulster in the mid-nineteenth Century.* Belfast: HMSO. [with extracts from original documents and full bibliography for vernacular building]

Gailey, A. 1984. *Rural Houses of the North of Ireland.* Edinburgh: John Donald. [the standard work on Ulster's vernacular traditions in building]

Galloway, P. 1992. *The Cathedrals of Ireland.* Belfast, Institute of Irish Studies.

Gould, M.H. 1983. *The Workhouses of Ulster.* Belfast: UAHS.

Guinness, D., and Ryan, W. 1971. *Irish Houses and Castles.* London: Irish Georgian Society. [includes plans and descriptions of several of Ulster's largest houses]

Hughes, K. and Hamlin A. 1997. *The Modern Traveller to the Early Irish Church.,* Dublin, Four Courts Press. [full section on buildings]

Jope, E.M. 1960. 'Fortification to Architecture in the North of Ireland', 1570-1700. *Ulster Journal of Archaeology,* 23. pp.97-123

Leask, H.G. 1951. *Irish Castles and Castellated Houses.* Dundalk: Dundalgan Press.

Leask, H.G. 1955, 1956 & 1960. *Irish Churches and Monastic Buildings.* 3 Vols. Dundalk: Dundalgan Press.

Mallory, J. P and McNeill, T.E. 1991. *The Archaeology of Ulster from Colonization to Plantation.* Belfast: Institute of Irish Studies, QUB.

McCutcheon, W.A. 1964. 'Ulster Railway Engineering and Architecture'. *Ulster Journal of Archaeology,* Vol. 27. pp.155-165

McCutcheon, W. A. 1980. *The Industrial Archaeology of Northern Ireland.* Belfast: HMSO.

McKinstry, R 1971. 'Contemporary Architecture' in *Causeway: The Arts in Ulster.* Dublin: Gill & Macmillan, pp.27-41.

McNeill, T. 1997. *Castles in Ireland.* London: Routledge.

McParland, E. 1989. *A Bibliography of Irish Architectural History.* Dublin: Irish Historical Studies.

McParland, E. 2001. *Public Architecture in Ireland 1680-1760.* New Haven; London: Yale University Press.

Meek, H.A. (ed.) 1966. *Ancient Monuments of Northern Ireland: Vol I: In State Care.* Belfast: HMSO, 1966

Meek, H.A. (ed.) 1969. *Ancient Monuments of Northern Ireland: Vol. II: Not in State Care.* Belfast: HMSO.

Oram, R. 2001. *Expressions of Faith: Ulster's Church Heritage.* Newtownards: Colourpoint.

Oram, R. 2007. 'Church buildings in Ireland, 1550-1850'. In *The Post-Medieval Archaeology of Ireland 1550-1850,* (eds) Horning A., O Baoill, R., Donnelly, C and Logue, P . Dublin, Wordwell, pp345-354. .

Potterton, H. 1975. *Irish Church Monuments, 1570-1880.* Belfast: UAHS.

Rankin, P., Dixon, H., and McKinstry, R. 1973. *Neo-classicism in Ulster.* Belfast: Arts Council of Northern Ireland. [illustrated account of the fashion for Neoclassical buildings in Ulster between about 1780 and 1840]

Reeves-Smyth, T. 2007. 'Community to privacy: late Tudor and Jacobean manorial architecture in Ireland, 1560-1640'. In *The Post-Medieval Archaeology of Ireland 1550-1850,* (eds) Horning A., O Baoill R., Donnelly, C and Logue, P . Dublin, Wordwell, 2007, pp289-326.

Shaffrey, P. 1975. *The Irish Town: an Approach to Survival.* Dublin: O'Brien Press.

BIBLIOGRAPHY

Stalley, R. 1971. *Architecture and Sculpture in Ireland 1150-1350*. Dublin: Gill & Macmillan.

Stalley, R. 1987. *The Cistercian Monasteries of Ireland: An Account of History, Art and Architecture of the White Monks in Ireland from 1142-1540.* New Haven; London: Yale University Press.

Walker. S. 2000. *Historic Ulster Churches.* Belfast, Institute of Irish Studies.

Wilkinson, G. 1845. *Practical Geology and Ancient Architecture of Ireland.* Dublin: Murray.

Wylie, R. 1997. *Ulster Model Schools: The Architecture and Fittings of Model National Schools Built in Ulster in the Nineteenth Century.* Belfast: UAHS.

Works on particular areas or buildings

Brett, C.E.B. 1967. *Buildings of Belfast 1700-1914.* London: Weidenfeld & Nicolson.

Brett, C.E.B. 1985. *Buildings of Belfast 1700-1914 2nd Edition.* Belfast: Friar's Bush Press.

Brett, C.E.B. 1996. *Buildings of Co. Antrim.* Belfast: UAHS.

Brett, C.E.B. 1999. *Buildings of Co. Armagh.* Belfast: UAHS.

Brett, C.E.B. 2002. *Buildings of North Co. Down.* Belfast: UAHS.

Brett, C.E.B., Gillespie, R. & Maguire, W.A. 2004. *Georgian Belfast, 1750-1850: Maps, Buildings and Trades.* Dublin: Royal Irish Academy.

Campbell, G. & Crowther, S. 1978. *Carrickfergus.* Belfast: UAHS.

Curl, J.S. 1979. *Moneymore and Draperstown: The Architecture and Planning of the Drapers' Company in Ulster.* Belfast: UAHS.

Curl, J.S. 1981. *The History, Architecture and Planning of The Fishmongers' Company in Ulster.* Belfast: UAHS.

Curl, J.S. 1986. *The Londonderry Plantation 1609-1914: The History, Architecture and Planning.* Chichester: Phillemore.

Dixon, H., Kenmuir, K. & Kennett, J. 1977. *Donaghadee and Portpatrick.* Belfast: UAHS.

Dufferin, Lord and Lady, Rankin, P., Stamp, G. & Maguire, W. 1985. *Clandeboye.* Belfast: UAHS.

Dunleath, Lord., Rowan, A.J., Malcolm, E. 1985. *Ballywalter Park.* Belfast: UAHS.

Evans, D.W. & Larmour, P. 1995. *Queens: An Architectural Legacy.* Belfast: Institute of Irish Studies.

Gallagher, L. 1995. *Grand Opera House, Belfast.* Belfast: Blackstaff.

Gallagher, L, & Rogers, R 1986. *Castle, Coast and Cottage: The National Trust in Northern Ireland.* Belfast: Blackstaff Press. Second edition 1992

Gillespie, R. & Royle, S.A. 2003. *Belfast: Part 1, to 1840.* Irish Historic Towns Atlas, 12.. Dublin: Royal Irish Academy.

Green, E.R.R. 1963. *Industrial Archaeology of Co. Down.* Belfast: HMSO.

Green, E.R.R. 1949. *The Lagan Valley 1800-1850.* London: Faber & Faber.

Hamond, F. 1991. *Antrim Coast and Glens Industrial Heritage.* Belfast: HMSO.

Hardy, P.D. (ed.) 2005. *Twenty-one Views of Belfast.* Belfast: Linen Hall Library & UAHS. [with notes and an introduction by CEB Brett]

Jocelyn, R., Earl of Roden. 2005. *Tollymore: The Story of an Irish Demesne.* Belfast: UAHS.

Jope, M (ed.) 1966. *Archaeological Survey of Co. Down.* Belfast: HMSO. largely written by D. M. Waterman, D.M. and A.E.P Collins, this book deals with field monuments and architecture in the county up to about 1840.

Kennedy, J., Woodman, G., Jupp, B., Mol, W. & Stelfox, D. 1999. *Parliament Buildings, Stormont.* Belfast: UAHS.

Kerrigan, P.M. 1995. Castles and Fortifications in Ireland. Cork.

Lacy, B (ed.) 1983. *Archaeological Survey of County Donegal.* Lifford: Donegal County Council. [includes castles, fortified houses and ecclesiastical sites]

Larmour, P. 1987. *Belfast: An Illustrated Architectural Guide.* Belfast: Friar's Bush Press.

Larmour, P. 1991. *The Architectural Heritage of Malone and Stranmillis.* Belfast: UAHS.

Larmour, P. 1992. *The Arts and Crafts Movement in Ireland.* Belfast: Friar's Bush Press.

Larmour, P. 1973. 'The turn of the century in Ulster: Art Nouveau and inventiveness' and 'Inter-War Architecture in Belfast'. *BigA,* 3, [magazine of Q.U.B. Department of Architecture]

Lewis-Crosby, J., Maguire, W., Rankin, P.,

BIBLIOGRAPHY

Nelson, C. & Jupp, B. 1993. *Hillsborough Castle*. Belfast: UAHS.

Lucey C. 2007. *The Stapleton Collection. Designs for the Irish Neoclassical Interior*. Tralee: Churchill House Press.

Maguire, W.A., Dixon, H., McKinstry, R., Wallace, C & Scott, R. 1983. *Malone House*. Belfast: UAHS.

McCracken, E. 1971. *The Palm House and Botanic Garden, Belfast*. Belfast: UAHS.

McCutcheon, W.A. 1963. 'The Newry Navigation: The Earliest Inland Canal in the British Isles.' *The Geographical Journal*, 129 4.. pp.466-480

McDonnell, H. 2004. *A History of Dunluce*. Belfast, Environment and Heritage Service.

McKinstry, R., Oram, R., Weatherup, R. & Wilson, P. 1992. *Armagh*. Belfast: UAHS.

McNeill, T. 1981. *Carrickfergus Castle*. Belfast: HMSO.

O'Reilly, S. 1998. *Irish Houses and Gardens. From the Archives of Country Life*. London: Aurum. [includes Caledon & Castle Coole]

Patton, M. 1993. *Central Belfast*. Belfast: UAHS.

Patton, M. 1999. *Bangor*. Belfast: UAHS.

Proctor, E.K 1832. *Belfast Scenery in Thirty Views, 1832*. Reprinted 1983 by the Linen Hall Library, Belfast [includes Proctor's engravings of Joseph Molloy's drawings of houses and their settings with modern commentary by Fred Heatley and Hugh Dixon]

Rankin, P.J. 1979. *Rathfriland and Hilltown*. Belfast: UAHS.

Reeves-Smyth. T. 1995. *Irish Castles*. Belfast: Appletree.

Reeves-Smyth, T., Oram, R. (eds) 2003. *Avenues to the Past: Essays Presented to Sir Charles Brett on his 75th Year*. Belfast: UAHS.

Rowan, A.J. 1979. *North West Ulster: the Counties of Londonderry, Donegal, Fermanagh and Tyrone*. New York: Penguin.

Sweetman, D. 1999. *The Medievals Castle of Ireland*. Cork: The Collins Press. [strangely does not cover in any detail the six counties of Northern Ireland)

Walker, B.M. & Dixon, H. (eds) 1983. *No Mean City: Belfast 1880-1914 in the Photographs of Robert French*. Belfast: Friar's Bush Press.

Walker, B.M. & Dixon, H. (eds) 1984. *In Belfast Town, 1864-1880: Early Photographs from the Lawrence Collection*. Belfast: Friar's Bush Press.

Ulster Architectural Heritage Society, Surveys and Lists of Historic Buildings published before 1975

Co. Antrim:

Girvan, D., Oram, R. Rowan, A.J 1970. *Antrim and Ballymena*. Belfast: UAHS.

Brett, C.E.B. 1972. *Glens of Antrim*. Belfast: UAHS.

Brett, C.E.B 1969. Lady Dunleath. *Lisburn*. Belfast: UAHS.

Girvan, W.D. 1972. *North Antrim*. Belfast: UAHS.

Brett, C.E.B. 1974. *Rathlin*. Belfast: UAHS.

Girvan, D., Rowan, A.J. 1970. *West Antrim*. Belfast: UAHS.

Co. Armagh:

Oram, R. 1971. *Craigavon*. Belfast: UAHS.

Co. Down:

Brett, C.E.B., Lady Dunleath. 1969. *Banbridge*. Belfast: UAHS.

Lady Dunleath, Rankin, P.J., Rowan, A.J. 1970. *Downpatrick*. Belfast: UAHS.

Brett, C.E.B. 1973. *East Down*. Belfast: UAHS.

Brett, C.E.B. 1974. *Mid Down*. Belfast: UAHS.

Rankin, P.J. 1975. *Mourne*. Belfast: UAHS.

Bell, G.P., Brett, C.E.B., Matthew, Sir R. 1969. *Portaferry and Strangford*. Belfast: UAHS.

Co. Fermanagh:

Dixon, H. 1973. *Enniskillen*. Belfast: UAHS.

Co. Londonderry:

Girvan, W.D. 1972. *Coleraine and Portstewart*. Belfast: UAHS.

Ferguson, W., Rowan, A.J., Tracey, J.J. 1970. *City of Derry*. Belfast: UAHS.

Girvan, W.D. 1975. *North Derry*. Belfast: UAHS.

Co. Monaghan:

Brett, C.E.B. 1970. Monaghan Town. Belfast: UAHS.

Co. Tyrone:

Oram, R., Rankin, P.J. 1971. *Dungannon and Cookstown*. Belfast: UAHS.

Belfast:

Brett, C.E.B., McKinstry, R. 1971. *Joy Street and Hamilton Street District*. Belfast: UAHS.

Rowan, A.J., Brett, C.E.B. 1975. *Queen's University Area.* Belfast: UAHS.

The National Trust and the Environment & Heritage Service publish guides to their properties.

Biographical works

With the honourable exception of Rolf Loeber's 1981. *Biographical Dictionary of Architects in Ireland 1600-1720* there is no easy way of finding out about individual architects. There are still only a handful of biographies and these must be supplemented with articles in journals and magazines, or passing mentions in the text or footnotes of books with wider subjects.

Loeber, Rolf. 1981. *A Biographical Dictionary of Architects in Ireland 1600-1720*, Murray, London. [architects and engineers involved in over thirty Ulster projects]

Blau, E.M. 1982. *Ruskinian Gothic: The Architecture of Deane and Woodward 1845-1861.* Ireland: Princeton University Press.

Brett, C.E.B 1976. *Roger Mulholland.* Belfast: UAHS.

Dixon, H. 1978. 'Honouring Thomas Jackson' in *Proceedings of Belfast Natural History and Philosophical Society.* 153rd Session 1974 2nd Series, 9, pp.23-31.

Dixon, H. 1974. 'W.H.Lynn' in *Irish Georgian Society Bulletin*, XVII, 1-2, Jan.

Dixon, H. 1978. *W.H.Lynn 1829-1915 Watercolours and Building Perspectives*, Belfast: Ulster Museum.

Dixon, H. 1976. *Soane and the Belfast Academical Institution.* Dublin: Gatherum.

Dunlop, D. 1868. The Life of William Barre. Belfast, Archer & Sons.

McParland, E. 1985. *James Gandon, Vitruvius Hibernicus.* London: Zwemmer.

McParland, E., Rowan, A.J. and Rowan, A.M. 1989. *The Architecture of Richard Morrison1767-1849. and William Vitruvius Morrison 1794-1838..* Dublin: The Irish Architectural Archive

Rankin, P. 1972. *Irish Building Ventures of the Earl Bishop of Derry.* Belfast: UAHS.

Sheehy, J. 1977. *J.J McCarthy and the Gothic Revival in Ireland.* Belfast: UAHS.

See also PADDI www.paddi.net for Paul Larmour's articles in *Perspective* on individual architects.

There is also much information about British architects who worked in Ulster in:-

Colvin, Howard. 1995. *A Biographical Dictionary of British Architects 1600-1840*, 3rd ed. [the principal work on the subject, but does not include those Irish architects who did not work in Great Britain]

Directory of British Architects 1834-1914 2001. London, Continuum. 2 Volumes. [Includes brief records for a number of Ulster architects with references to RIBA holdings]

Ware, Dora. 1976. *A Short Dictionary of British Architects* [includes brief lives for many post-1840 architects who did work in Ulster]

Journals

The following contain much information about Ulster buildings:-

The Architect 1869- . and *Building News* 1855- . were united in 1926

The Builder 1843- .

Country Life 1897- .

Dublin then *Irish Builder* 1859- .

Irish Arts Review 1984-.

Irish Georgian Society Bulletin 1958- ., re-named *Irish Architectural and Decorative Studies* 1998- .

Journal of Royal Society of Antiquaries of Ireland 1851- .

Perspective 1992- .

Ulster Architect 1984- .

Ulster Folk Life 1955- .

Ulster Journal of Archaeology first series, 1853-1862; second series, 1895-1911; third series, 1938- .

General and Comparative Works – with Ulster references

AA Illustrated Road Book of Ireland. 1956.. Dublin: Automobile Association. Second illustrated edition 1966 [full of good line drawings of a wide range of buildings; dating and attributions of mixed reliability; original photographs on which drawings were based are now housed in the Irish Architectural Archive, Dublin].

Archer, L. 1999. *Architecture in Britain and Ireland 600-1500.* London: Harvill Press.

Becker, A, Olley, J. & Wang, W. (eds) 1997. *20th Century Architecture Ireland.* Munich; New York: Prestel.

Craig, M.J., and the Knight of Glin. 1970. *Ireland Observed.* Cork: Mercier. [a gazetteer of major buildings of all periods, particularly important for the classical tradition]

Craig, M.J. 1978. *Architecture in Ireland.*

BIBLIOGRAPHY

Dublin: Department of Foreign Affairs.

Craig, M.J. 1982. *The Architecture of Ireland from the Earliest Times to 1880.* London: Batsford.

Craig, M.J. 1992. *Dublin, 1600-1860.* Dublin: Penguin.

Cruickshank, D. 1985. *Guide to the Georgian Buildings of Britain and Ireland.* London: Weidenfeld & Nicholson.

Curl, J.S. 2006. *Oxford Dictionary of Architecture and Landscape Architecture.* 2nd ed. Oxford: Oxford University Press.

Curl, J.S. 2007. *Victorian Architecture: Diversity and Invention.* Reading, Spire.

De Breffny, B. 1975. *The Churches and Abbeys of Ireland.* London: Thames and Hudson.

De Breffny, B. 1977. *Castles of Ireland.* London: Thames and Hudson.

Fleming, J., Honour, H. and Pevsner, N. 1998. *The Penguin Dictionary of Architecture and Landscape Architecture.* 5th Ed. Harmondsworth: Penguin.

Girouard, M. 1992. *Town and Country.* London; New Haven: Yale University Press.

Harbison, P. 1970. *Guide to the National Monuments in the Republic of Ireland.* Dublin: Gill & Macmillan. [includes entries on the major monuments of Cavan, Donegal and Monaghan]

Howley, J. 1993. *The Follies and Garden Buildings of Ireland.* New Haven: Yale University Press.

Killanin, M. & Duignan, M. 1989. *Shell Guide to Ireland.* Dublin: Gill & Macmillan, [contains a wide range of architectural information]

McCullough, N. 1987. *A Lost Tradition: The Nature of Architecture in Ireland.* Dublin: Gandon Editions.

McEldowney, M., Murray, M., Murtagh, B. & Sterrett, K. (eds) 2005. *Planning in Ireland and Beyond: Essays in Honour of John V Greer.* Belfast: Queen's University Belfast.

Rothery, S. 1991. *Ireland and the New Architecture 1900-1940.* Dublin, Lilliput Press.

Rothery, S. 1997. *A Field Guide to the Buildings of Ireland: Illustrating the Smaller Buildings of Town and Countryside.* Dublin, Lilliput Press.

Shaffrey, P. 1984. *Irish Countryside Buildings: Everyday Architecture in the Rural Landscape.* Dublin: O'Brien Press.

Shaffrey, P. & Shaffrey, M. 1983. *Buildings of Irish Towns: Treasures of Everyday Architecture.* Dublin: O'Brien Press.

Simms, A. & Andrews, J.H. (eds) 1984. *Irish Country Towns.* Ireland: Mercier Press.

Williams, J.A. 1994. *Companion Guide to Architecture in Ireland 1837-1921.* Blackrock: Irish Academic Press.

Index

N.I. = Northern Ireland; italicised page numbers refer to illustrations

abbeys 12, 32–3
Academic Tudor 148–9
Adam, Robert 112, 118, 133
Albert Memorial Clock Tower (Belfast) *127*, *162*
Alexander Crescent (Armagh) *200*
Alexander Memorial Cottages (Londonderry) 200
almshouses 148
Altnagelvin Hospital (Londonderry) 203
Anderson and McAuley's store (Belfast) *172*
Antrim, Co.
    barn churches 77
    bawns 58, 59
    castles 47, 132, 133
    churches 45, 95, 160, *181*, 206
    country houses 98, 99
    friaries 35
    gentleman's 'vernacular' 114
    Gothick cottage 110
    high houses 64
    lockkeepers' houses 96
    mansions 143, 144
    mausoleums 118
    meeting houses 124–5
    natural fortresses 37
    plantation churches 66
    prehistoric 20
    railway stations 156, 157
    round towers 25
    viaducts 141
    Victorian churches 139
Antrim County Hall *205*
Antrim Court House 90, *91*, 92
Antrim Parish Church 42, *43*

Archbishop Robinson's Chapel (Co. Armagh) 119
Ardglass Bay (Co. Down) 40
Ardress House (Co. Armagh) *112*, 113
Argory mansion (Co. Armagh) 120
Armagh, Co.
    banks, Italianate 150
    castles 134, 135
    churches 119, 122, 206
    earthworks 22
    farmhouses, gentlemen's 113
    forts 50
    gentleman's 'vernacular' 115
    houses *200*, 208
    mansions 120, 145
    Palladianism 106
    post-restoration houses 72
    public buildings 136
    railway bridges 141
    ring forts 23
    Victorian churches 138, 139
Armagh Court House *136*, 137
Armagh town 24, 27
Armagh U.D.C. 200
Art Deco 189, 192–3, 196
Art Nouveau 172, 178–81, 184
Arts and Crafts 157, 184–5, 188
Ashby Institute (Queen's University, Belfast) *202*, 203
Audley's Castle (Co. Down) 38
Augher Castle (Co. Tyrone) 54
Austin & Co., Ltd. (Londonderry) *182*, 183

Balfour Castle (Co. Fermanagh) 54
Balleeghan church windows (Co. Donegal) 42
Ballycopeland Windmill (Co. Down) 97

Ballygally Castle (Co. Antrim) *64*, 65
Ballykeel Portal Dolmen (Co. Armagh) *20*, 21
Ballykelly (Co. Londonderry) 60
Ballyscullion house (Co. Londonderry) 117
Ballyvester (Co. Down), house at 81
Ballywalter Park mansion (Co. Down) *142*, 143
Ballywatt Presbyterian Church (Co. Antrim) *181*
Banagher Church (Co. Londonderry) 26, *27*
Bangor (Co. Down) 24, 25
Bangor Old Custom House (Co. Down) *65*, 68
Bank Building (Castle Place, Belfast) *182*
Bank of Ireland (Newtownards, Co. Down) *187*
Bank of Ireland (Royal Avenue, Belfast) *192*
banks 14, 150–5
barn churches 76–7
baronial style 65
Baronscourt mansion (Co. Tyrone) 120, 128
barracks 46
Barre, W.J. 152
Barry, Charles 143
Batt, William 166
Bauhaus 202
bawns 58–9, *60*, 70
Belfast
    and Art Nouveau 178–81
    churches 117, 159, 161
    commercial buildings 164, 172, 182, 192, 193
    concrete and brick sculptural buildings 204
    Crown Bar *169*
    factories 194
    Giant's Ring 21
    Grand Opera House *168*
    hospitals 200
    houses 184, 185
    monuments 162
    official buildings 186, *188*, 189
    public buildings 137, 196–9
    railway stations 156
    and Ruskinian Gothic 154
    schools and colleges 148–9, 197, 202–3, *208*
    Victorian engineering 140
Belfast (Northern) Bank (Newtownards, Co. Down) 154, *155*
Belfast Academical Institution 137
Belfast Academy 148
Belfast Bank (Armagh) *150*
Belfast City Hall *170*, 171
Belfast Municipal Museum 186
Bell, G.P. 200
Bellaghy vintners (Co. Londonderry) 60
Bellamont Forest house (Co. Cavan) *15*, *104*, 105
Beltany, Co. Donegal 21
Benburb (Co. Tyrone) 58
Bernard, Walter 22
Berwick Hall (Co. Down) 80
Blackwood and Jury 178, 179, 180, 194
Blessingbourne house (Co. Tyrone) 115
Boddie, C.L. 195
Bogay house (Co. Donegal) 86
Bonamargy Friary (Co. Antrim) *35*

217

INDEX

Botanic Primary School (Belfast) 197
Bowden, John 136
bridges 194
Brownlow House (Co. Armagh) 145–7
Buncrana Castle (Co. Donegal) 84, 85
Burkitt, J. 195
Burman and Goodall 205
Burrenwood Cottage (Co. Down) 115
Burt Castle (Co. Donegal) 55
Byrne, Barry 192
Byrne, E & J 168

cabins 78
Caledon mansion (Co Tyrone) 120, 130
Carrickfergus (Co. Antrim) 50–1, 52
Carrickfergus Castle (Co. Antrim) 47
Castle, Richard 94, 96, 106, 107
Castle Buildings (Belfast) 177, 178, 179
Castle Caulfield (Co. Tyrone) 54, 56
Castle Coole (Co. Fermanagh) 86, 87, 120, 121, 130, 131
Castle Hume (Co. Fermanagh) 106
castle style 134–5
Castle Upton (Co. Antrim) 133
Castle Ward mansion (Co. Down) 108, 109
Castlefergus Castle 46
castles 28–31, 36, 40–1, 46, 58–9, 60
castles, symmetrical 133
cathedrals 34, 46
    Gothic revival 159

Cavan, Co. 15, 27, 104, 184
Cavan Court House 137
Cavan Town Hall 184
Celtic revival 25, 160–1
chapels 119
Charlemont fort (Co. Armagh) 50, 51
Chichester, Arthur 51, 52
Chichester Monument 52
Christian, early 22–5
churches
    Art Nouveau 180–1
    barn 76–7
    Board of First Fruits 14
    Celtic revival 160–1
    early Georgian 94–5
    early Victorian 138–9
    Georgian 122–3
    Georgian Gothick 110
    Gothic revival 159
    Grey Abbey (Co. Down) 12
    late medieval windows 43
    medieval survival 44–5
    Neoclassical 137
    plantation 66–7
    Presbyterian 124, 125, 139
    Romanesque style 26, 27
    Ruskinian Gothic 154
    symbolical sculptural 206–7
    transitional style 33
Clady Cottage (Co. Antrim) 114
Clandeboye (Co. Down) 128
Clarence Place Hall (Belfast) 154
Classical revival 116
Classical tradition 12
    Belfast as 'Athens of the North' 137
    at Castle Upton (Co. Antrim) 133
    in Elizabethan revival 144
    in Georgian churches 122

in official buildings 186–7
and plantation city defence 63
in Victorian churches 138
Clough (Co. Down) 29
Clough Motte and Castle (Co. Down) 29
Coalisland Canal Aqueduct (Co. Tyrone) 97
coastguard stations 14
Colebrooke mansion (Co. Fermanagh) 120, 128, 129
Coleraine station (Co. Londonderry) 156
Colville, Alexander 70
commercial buildings 164–5, 182–3
concrete framed buildings 194–5
convent chapel (Enniskillen, Co. Fermanagh) 194
Cooley, Thomas 119, 122
Cormac's Chapel (Cashel, Co. Tipperary) 160–1
Corratory Bridge (Co. Tyrone) 195
Corry, Isaac 114
cottages 110, 115
Cottingham, L.N. 45, 139
country houses 98–103
court houses 14, 60, 92–3, 136–7
    Ruskinian Gothic 154
court tombs 21
Cowd Castle (Co. Down) 40
Craig, Maurice 16
Craig, Vincent 178, 180, 181
Craigmore-Mullaghglass viaduct 157
crannogs 23
Creggandevesky court tomb, Co. Tyrone 21
Crookedstone house (Co. Antrim) 81

Crown Bar (Belfast) 169
Cruickshank and Seward 203
Crum (Crom) Castle (Co. Fermanagh) 85
Crymble's music shop (Belfast) 178
Culfeitrim Church (Co. Antrim) 42, 43
Culmore Fort (Co. Londonderry) 63
Cunningham, William 74
Curl, James Stevens 16
Curle, John 87

'Dallas' (Malone Road, Belfast) 184, 185
Dallywaye, John 58
Dalway's Bawn (Co. Antrim) 58, 59
Dance the Younger, George 128
De Rose, Levan 50
defences, plantation city 62–3
Derry Churches (Co. Down) 26
Derrygonnelly church (Co. Fermanagh) 66
Derrymore house (Co. Armagh) 114, 115
Derrywoone Castle (Co, Tyrone) 54, 55, 57
Devenish Church (Co. Fermanagh) 42
Devenish monastery (Co. Fermanagh) 24, 25
Diestelkamp, Edward 16
dolmens 20, 21
Donaghadee Harbour Lighthouse (Co. Down) 140
Donaghadee motte (Co. Down) 28
Donegal, Co.
    castles 55
    churches 161, 180, 208

218

INDEX

country houses 84, 85, 86, 88
gabled strong houses 68
hostels 194
houses 185
monuments 52
Romanesque style 27
round towers 25
stone circles 21
Donegal Castle 54
Doohat strong house
(Co. Fermanagh) 68
Dorsey earthworks
(Co. Armagh) 22
double-pile houses 70–1
Down, Co.
   barn churches 77
   castles 30, 31, 40
   churches 83, 95, 122, 123
   country houses 98
   Downpatrick Assembly
     Rooms 166
   early Georgian 90
   gatehouses 111
   gentleman's 'vernacular' 115
   Georgian Gothick 108, 110
   Gothic Revival 158
   Gothic style 34
   Grey Abbey (Co. Down) 12
   high houses 65
   Hill Hall Church *180*
   houses 184, *201*, 201, 203
   houses, planters' 80
   lighthouses 140
   mansions 120, 128, 142, 143, 145
   monasteries 24
   monuments 162–3
   Mount Stewart 17
   Neoclassicism 116
   New Forge House 13
   Norman mottes 28, 29
   Palladianism 107

   plantation classicism 52, 53
   post-restoration houses 72, 73
   railway stations 157
   ring forts 23
   Rosemount House, Grey
     Abbey 14
   temples 118
   tower houses 38
   Victorian churches 139
   Waringstown *11*, 12, 72, *73*, 80
   windmills 97
Down and Connor Church
Architecture Society 158
Downhill demesne
(Co. Londonderry) 117
Downpatrick Assembly Rooms
(Co. Down) 166
Downpatrick church (Co.
Down) 27
Dromena Cashel (Co. Down) 23
Dromore motte (Co. Down) 28
Dromore vernacular house
(Co. Tyrone) *79*
Dromore viaduct (Co. Down) 157
Drum Bridge Lock Keeper's
House (Co. Antrim) *96*
Drumbo round tower (Co.
Down) 25
Ducart, Davis 96
Duff, Thomas 137, 145, 158
Dunbar, John 66
Dundarave mansion (Co.
Antrim) *143*
Dundonald castle (Co. Down) 28
Dundonald House (Co. Down) *202*, 203
Dundrum Castle (Co. Down) 30

Duneigh Motte (Co. Down) *28*
Dungannon (Co. Tyrone), bank 154
Dungannon Castle (Co. Tyrone) 37
Dungannon Court House 136
Dungiven Castle
(Co. Londonderry) *133*
Dunluce Castle (Co. Antrim) 36
Dunminning Cottage
(Co. Antrim) *110*
Dunseverick castle (Co. Antrim) 37

earthworks 21, 22, 28, 30
Ecclesiastical Commissioners 14, 136, 161
Echlinville house (Co. Down) 72, *73*
Edwardian style 182–3
Egyptian Arch (Co. Armagh) 141
Elizabethan revival 144, 145, 157
Elmgrove school (Belfast) 197
engineering
   Georgian 96–7
   Victorian 140–1
Enniskillen Court House 137
Enniskillen Town Hall (Co.
Fermanagh) 166, *167*
Ensor, George 112
Ewart's store (Belfast) *164*

Faith Mission Hall (Co. Antrim) *138*, 139
farmhouses, gentlemen's 112–3
Farrell, William 128, 137
Fennell, W.J. 200
Fermanagh, Co.
   bridges 194

   castles 54
   chapels 194
   country houses 85, 86
   early Georgian 90
   Enniskillen Town Hall 166, *167*
   gabled strong houses 68
   houses 184
   mansions 120, 128
   monasteries 24
   Palladianism 106
   plantation churches 67
   railway stations 156
   Regency style 130
Ferris Wheel (Belfast) *210*
First Fruits, Board of 14
Flamboyant style 42
Florence Court (Co.
Fermanagh) 100, *101*–3, 120
follies 108
fortresses, natural 36–7
Franciscan Friary (Armagh) 33
'freestyle', Edwardian 182

Galgorm Castle (Co. Antrim) 66, *70*
gaols 14, 148
garden buildings 108
Garnier, Tony 202
gatehouses 38, 63, 110, 145
gentleman's 'vernacular' 114–5
Georgian, early 81
   churches 94–5
   country houses 84–9
   doors 90–1
   public buildings 92–3
Georgian, late 128–9
Georgian, mid- 98–103
Georgian engineering 96–7
Georgian meeting houses 124–5
Giant's Ring 21

INDEX

Gibbs, James 93, 107, 189
Gibbsian decoration 93, 122, 124
Gibson and Taylor 203
Gill Hall (Co Down) 90, 91, *91*
Glenarm Castle (Co. Antrim) *144*, 145
Glendun viaduct (Co. Antrim) 141
Glenmakieran House (Hollywood, Co Down) 184, *185*
Gordon, Stewart 133
Gosford Castle (Co. Armagh) *135*
Gothic revival 158–9, 188
Gothic style
    asymmetric castle 132
    in churches 160
    Inch Abbey (Co. Down) 33
    monasteries 34–5
    Newry Presbyterian Church 139
    railway stations 156
    Ruskinian 154–5
    St. Columb's Cathedral (Londonderry) 63
    St. John's Church (Lisnadill, Co.Armagh) 122
    Wray Castle (Co. Donegal) 69
Gothick, Georgian 108–11, 122, 138
Grand Opera House (Belfast) *168*
Grange at Waringstown (Co. Down) 81
Great Victoria Street station (Belfast) 156
Greencastle Norman hall (Co. Down) *31*
Grey Abbey (Co. Down) *12*

Greyabbey (Co. Down) 108
Grianan of Aileach (Co. Donegal) 22
Gropius, Walter 202

Hall Craig (Co. Fermanagh) 90
Hamilton, James 164
Hamilton, Malcolm 54
Hanna, Denis O'D. 206
Hargrave, John 136
'Haslemere' (Belfast) 185
Hastings, William 165
HEARTH 16
Helen's Bay railway station (Co. Down) *157*
Hennebique, François 194
Henry O'Hara's Castle (Co. Londonderry) 133
Hevey, Timothy 161, 163
Hezlett House (Co. Londonderry) *78*, 79
Hiberno-Romanesque 160
High Victorian style 162–3
hill forts 22
Hill Hall Church (Co. Down) *180*
Hillsborough church (Co. Down) 77, 110
Hillsborough Fort Gatehouse (Co. Down) *111*
Holy Trinity Church (Co. Antrim) 94, *95*
Hopper, Thomas 135
hostel (Lough Derg, Co. Donegal) 194
houses 11, 14, *60*, 107, 112–5, 143
    20th century 200–1
    Arts and Crafts 184–5
    castle style 134–5
    cruck-built 79
    double-pile 70–1

    fortified 54
    gabled strong 68–9
    planters' 80–1
    post-restoration 72–3
    Ruskinian Gothic 154
    Scottish high 64–5
    timber-frame 60
    vernacular 78–9
    William and Mary 74–5
    yeoman's 80–1
Housing Executive, N.I. 16, 201, 208
huts, prehistoric 20

Inch Abbey (Co. Down) *33*
Inch House (Co. Donegal) 85
infirmaries 14
Inishkerragh bridge (Co. Fermanagh) 194
International Style 202–3, 204–5
Iron Age 22–5
Italian Mannerism 150–1

Jackson, Thomas 137, 159
Jacobean style 53, 88, 128, 148
Jacobethan mansions 144–7
Jazz Age Modern 192
Johnston, Francis 119, 120, 137
Jordan's Castle (Co. Down) 38, *40*
Joymount (Co. Armagh) *50*
Jury, Percy Morgan 178

Keane, J.B. 133
Kilclief Castle (Co. Down) 38, *39*
Killevy (Co. Armagh) 26, *134*
Killyhevlin House (Enniskillen, Co. Fermanagh) 184
Killymoon Castle (Co. Tyrone) *132*, 135

Kilmore Cathedral (Co. Cavan) *26*, 27
Kinbane Castle, Cregganboy (Co. Antrim) 37
Kilmore Church (Co. Down) 122, *123*
Kilwaughter house (Co. Antrim) 132
Kinbane
King's Hall (Belfast) 196, *198–9*
Kirkiston Castle (Co. Down) *41*
Knight, Richard Payne 132
Knockbreda church (Co. Antrim) 77

Lady Anne's Temple, Castle Ward (Co. Down) 118
Lagan Navigation 96–7
Lanyon, Charles 143, 148, 149, 150, 151
Larmour, Paul 16
Laurentian Library (Florence) 53
Le Corbusier 202
Legananny Portal Dolmen (Co. Down) *21*
Leslie Hill (Co. Antrim) 98, *99*
Letterkenny Court House 136
Lifford Church monument (Co. Donegal) 52
Lifford Court House (Co. Donegal) *93*
lighthouses 140–1
Linsfort Castle (Inishowen, Co. Donegal) 85
Lisbellaw station (Co. Fermanagh) 156
Lisburn station (Co. Antrim) 156
Lisnagade raths (Co. Armagh) *23*
Lissan Rectory (Co. Fermanagh) 130

INDEX

lockkeepers' houses 96–7
Londonderry, Co.
    churches 139, *181*
    city walls 63
    commercial buildings 182
    country houses 88
    hospitals 203
    houses 78, 200
    Neoclassicism 117
    Picturesque style 133
    plantation settlement 60, 61
    railway stations 156
    Romanesque style 27
    schools and colleges 148
Londonderry City walls *62*, *63*
Londonderry Court House 136
Londonderry Waterside station 156
Lutyens, Sir Edwin 185
Lynn, William Henry 154, 160, 182
Lytle's store (Belfast) 164

M2 Motorway (Greencastle, Co. Antrim) 204–5
MacGeagh, John 197
Magdalen College (Oxford) 148
Magee College (Londonderry) 148
Maghera church (Co. Derry) 27
Magheramena Castle (Co. Fermanagh) 133
Mannerism 53
manor houses 37, 144–7
mansions 108, 120–1, 128–9, 142–3
markets 60
Martin Memorial (Shrigley, Co. Down) 162, *163*
masonic hall (Enniskillen, Co. Fermanagh) *196*

Matcham, Frank 168
Mater Hospital (Belfast) 200
Maufe, Edward 197
mausoleums *118*
McAdam Design Partnership 201
McCarthy, James 159
McCausland's (Belfast) *165*
McCausland's store (Belfast) 164
McConnell, Dixon & Downes 192
McCormick, Liam, and Partners 209
McKnight, Gordon 206
McNeill, T.E. 16
McParland, Edward 16
medieval period 42–5
medieval tradition 46–7, 63
meeting houses 77, 124–5
Mercer's house (Co. Londonderry) *61*
Methodist Church (Portstewart, Co. Londonderry) 139
Methodist College (Belfast) 148
Michelangelo 53
Middle Church (Co Antrim) 76
Modern Movement 184, 186
modern style 192
modernistic functional 196–9
Moira Station (Co. Antrim) 156
Monaghan, Co. 120
Monaghan Court House 136, *210*
monasteries 24
Monea Castle (Co. Fermanagh) *54*
monuments 162–3
Moore, H. Armytage 190
Morris, William 184
Morrison, William V. 17, 128, 144, 145

mottes 28
Mouchel, Louis 194
Mount Panther mansion (Co. Down) 9
Mount Stewart mansion (Co. Down) *17*, 128
Mountsandel, Co. Antrim 20
Moyry Fort (Co. Armagh) 50
Mulholland, Roger 124
Munce and Kennedy 206, 207
museums 123, *186*
Music Department (Stranmillis College, Belfast) *204*
Mussenden Temple (Co. Londonderry) *117*
Myers, Christopher 96

Narrow Water Castle (Co. Down) 38, *40*, 145
Nash, John 115, 130, 132
Nash, Robert 132
Navan Fort 22
Necarne Castle (Co. Fermanagh) 133
Nendrum (Co. Down) *25*
Nendrum monastery (Co. Down) 24
Neoclassicism 116–9, 128, 132, 142
    mansions 120–1
    public buildings 136–7
Neo-Georgian buildings 188–91, 196
Neville's Town Hall (Londonderry) 63
New Forge House (Magheralin, Co. Down) *13*, 15
New Victoria College (Belfast) *208*
Newark Castle (Co. Down) *40*
Newcomen, Robert 71
Newry Cathedral (Co. Down) 159

Newry Navigation 96
Newtownards Priory (Co. Down) 34, 52
Newtownbreda Parish Church (Co. Antrim) 94, *95*
Newtownbutler station (Co. Fermanagh) 156
Newtownstewart house (Co. Tyrone) *71*
Norman period 28–31
Northern Bank (Belfast) *151*

Oakfield (Co. Donegal) *87*
Oakfield House (Co. Donegal) 86
Ocean Building (Belfast) 182
O'Dubigan, Matthew 42
official buildings 186–7
Old Library (Queen's University, Belfast) 154
Old Museum Building (Belfast) *137*
Omagh Court House (Co. Tyrone) 136
Omer, Thomas 96

Palladianism 104–7, 109, 118, 172, 189
Palladio, Andrea 98, 104, 116
Palm House (Botanic Gardens, Belfast) 140, *141*
Papworth, George 134
Parliament Buildings (Stormont, Belfast) 189, *190*
passage graves 21
Paxton, Sir Joseph 140
Pearce, Sir Edward Lovett 15, 96, 104, 106
Pembroke Castle (Wales) 30
Perpendicular style 42
Phillips's market house (Londonderry) 63

INDEX

Picturesque movement 132–3
plantation classicism 52–3
plantation villages *61*
Playfair, William H. 145
police station (Seaforde, Co. Down) *189*
Poor Law Commissioners 14
Port Hall (Co. Donegal) 88, *89*, 93
portal dolmens 20, 21
Portinode bridge (Co Fermanagh) 194, *195*
Portrush station (Co. Antrim) 157
Portstewart Presbyterian Church (Co. Londonderry) *181*
Prehen house (Co. Londonderry) *88*
prehistory 20–1
Preston, John 131
Priestly, Michael 88, 89, 93
Provincial Bank (Castle Place, Belfast) *152*, *153*
public buildings 136–7, 154
    Victorian 166–7
Pugin, Augustus 139, 158
Purdysburn Village (Co. Down) 201
Pym, Francis 186, 204, 205

Queen Anne style 87, 120
Queen's College (Belfast) 148, *149*

railway stations 14, 140–1, 156–7
    Ruskinian Gothic 154
Randalstown viaduct (Co. Antrim) 157
Raphoe church (Co. Donegal) 27, 161
raths *23*

Raven, Thomas 62
rectories 130
Red Hall (Co. Antrim) 88, *89*
Regency style 115, 128, 130–1, 189
religious houses 34
Renaissance 50–1, 52, 63, 66
Rennie, John 140
Revett, Nicholas 116
Richhill Castle (Co. Armagh) *72*
ring forts 23
Rippingham, T.F.O. 188, 189
Robinson, M.A. 182, *183*
Robinson, Peter Frederick 128
Robinson and Cleaver's store (Belfast) 164
Rococo 109, 112
Roe Park (Co. Londonderry) 107
Roman Imperial decoration 118
Romanesque style 25, 26–7, 30, 32
Romano, Giulio 151
Roome, W.J.W. 178, 194
Rosemary Street meeting house (Belfast) 124–5
Rosemount House (Grey Abbey, Co. Down) 14
Rossmore Memorial (Monaghan) 162
Rostrevor (Co. Down), houses in cottage style 115
Roughan Castle (Co. Tyrone) 54
round towers 25
Rowan, Alistair 16
Royal Courts of Justice (Belfast) 189, *191*
Ruskin, John 152, 160
Ruskinian Gothic 154–5

St. Columba's Church (Co. Armagh) *206*
St. Columb's Cathedral (Londonderry) 63
St. Doulough Church (Co. Dublin) 160
St. George's Church (Belfast) 117
St. John's Church (Lisnadill, Co. Armagh) *122*
St. John's Church (Moira, Co. Down) *83*, 90–1
St. John's Point (Co. Down) 26
St. Malachy's Church (Belfast) 159
St. Mary's Abbey Church (Co. Fermanagh) *42*
St. Matthew's Church (Woodvale Road, Belfast) *161*
St. Michael's Church (Creeslough, Co. Donegal), 208, *209*
St. Nicholas Church (Co. Antrim) *45*
St. Nicholas church (Co. Antrim) 52
St. Patrick and Colman's Cathedral (Newry, Co. Down) 158
St. Patrick and Colman's cathedral (Newry, Co. Down) *159*
St. Patrick's Cathedral (Armagh) *44*
St. Patrick's cathedral (Armagh) 139, *158*
St. Patrick's Cathedral (Dundalk) 158
St. Patrick's church (Co. Tyrone) *161*
St. Patrick's Church (Jordanstown, Co. Antrim) *160*
Saintfield House (Co. Down) 98
schools and colleges 148–9, 154
Scotch Church (Co. Armagh) 138, *139*

Scott, J. 192, 193
Scott, William 166, 184, 194
Scottish Mutual Building (Belfast) 182
Scottish Provident Institution (Belfast) 172, *173*–5
Sculptural style
    concrete and brick 204–5
    symbolical 206–7
    topographical 208–9
Seaforde mansion (Co. Down) 120, 128, *129*
Seaver, Henry 182
See House mansion (Co. Monaghan) 120
Serlio, Sebastiano 116
settlements, plantation 60–1
Seymour Hill Church (Co. Antrim) 206, *207*
Shane's Castle (Co. Antrim) 132
Shanks, Donald 202
Shanks & Leighton 208
Sharman D. Neill building (Belfast) 178
Shaw, James 64
Sheehy, Jeanne 16
Shore Cottages (Portaferry, Co. Down) *201*
Sinclair's store (Belfast) 192, *193*
Sion House (Sion Mills, Co. Tyrone) *184*
Skinners at Dungiven and Brackfield (Co. Londonderry) 60
Smith, Ronald Ingleby 188
Soane, John 120, 128, 137
Somerset's Linen Factory (Belfast) *194*
Southwell Charity (Co. Down) *107*
Spa (Ballynahinch, Co. Down) 110

INDEX

Springhill house (Co. Londonderry) *74, 75*
St. John's Church (Moira, Co. Down) *94*
stable blocks 107
Stalley, Roger 16
Stapleton, Michael 112, 113
stone circles 21
Stranmillis College (Belfast) *188*
Stuart, James 'Athenian' 116
Sullivan, Louis 202
Swann, J.H. 202
symbolical sculptural style 206–7

Tandragee (Co. Armagh) 208
Temple Finghin (Co. Offaly) 161
Temple of the Winds (Co. Down) *116*
temples 118
Templeton Mausoleum (Co. Antrim) *118*
terraces *106*, 154
Tesco (Castle Place, Belfast) *152, 153*
The Fort (Co. Down) 110
theatres 168–9
Thomas, Sir Alfred Brumwell 170
Thornley, Sir Arnold 189, 190
Tollymore Park (Co. Down) 108
topographical sculptural style 208–9
Tory Island (Co. Donegal) 25
tower, square 50
tower houses 38–41, 51, 68
towers 29
town halls 154
toy Gothick 122
Tranarossan Youth Hostel (Co. Donegal) 185

transitional style 32–3
Trinity Presbyterian Church (Letterkenny, Co. Donegal) 180
Tudor Revival 13, 42, 144, 145, 159
Tudor style 14
Tulloch, Frederick 185
Tully Castle (Co. Fermanagh) 54, *55*
Tullynakill Church (Co. Fermanagh) *67*
Turkish baths 148
Turner, Richard 140
Tyrone, Co.
    aqueducts 97
    bawns 58
    bridges 194–5
    churches 161
    court houses 136
    court tombs 21
    double-pile houses 71
    fortified houses 54, 55, 56, 57
    gentleman's 'vernacular' 115
    houses *184*
    mansions 120
    natural fortresses 37
    Picturesque style 132
    Regency style 130
Tyrone Canal 96

Ulster College of Art (Belfast) *202*, 203
Ulster Folk and Transport Museum (Co. Down) 123
Ulster Museum (Belfast) *186*, 204, *205*
Unsworth, William 184

van der Rohe, Mies 202
Vaughan, John 84
Venetian style 154
vernacular architecture 13, 80–1

viaducts 157
Vicar's Hill Terrace (Co. Armagh) *106*
Victorian, late
    commercial buildings 172–5
    public buildings 170–1
Victorian architecture 138–9
    commercial 164–5
    engineering 140–1
    High 152–3
    Italianate mansions 142–3
    Jacobethan mansions 144–7
    public buildings 166–7
Voysey, Charles Francis Annesley 184

Wales 30, 63
walls, city *62*
Walpole, Horace (4th Earl of Orford) 108
warehouses 154
Waringstown mansion (Co. Down) *11, 12*, 72, *73*, 80
Water Office (Belfast) 154
Watt, Tulloch and Fitzsimons 185
Welland, Joseph 136, 210
Welland & Gillespie 161
West, J.G. 189
West, Robert 100
White House (Co. Down) 68
Whitla Hall, Sir William (Queen's University, Belfast) *197*
Wilkinson, George 14, 15, 148
William and Mary 74–5, 86
Wilshere, R.S. 197
Wingfield, Richard 58–9
Wolfenden Monument (Co. Down) *53*
Woodgate, Robert 128
workhouses 14, 148

Wray Castle (Co. Donegal) 68, 69
Wright, Frank Lloyd 202
Wyatt, James 120
Wynnes, J.C. 186

Yorke, Rosenberg and Mardell 203
Young and Mackenzie 172, 182
youth hostels 185

223

Acknowledgements

Monaghan Court House, Monaghan (1829, Joseph Welland) with Hanoverian Coat of Arms.

This book contains 223 illustrations, of which 211 are photographs, many taken especially for this book on behalf of the Ulster Architectural Heritage Society. The society is indebted to the following for supplying illustrations: To A.C. Merrick for the front and back dust-jacket & pages 11, 12, 13, 14, 15, 17, 26, 27, 35, 41, 42, 43a, 43b, 44, 53, 64, 68, 69, 70, 72, 73a, 76, 77, 83, 84, 85a, 88, 89a, 91a, 92, 93, 94, 95a, 95b, 96, 99, 104, 105, 106, 107, 110, 111, 116, 118, 121, 123, 124, 125, 128, 129a, 132, 133, 136, 137, 138, 139, 140, 142, 145a, 148, 149, 150, 151, 154, 157, 158a, 158b, 161b, 163, 166, 167, 180, 183, 186, 187, 188, 189, 190, 194, 196, 197, 198-9, 200, 201, 203, 204, 205a, 205b, 206, 207, 208, 209, 224; To the Environment and Heritage Service and their photographers Gail Pollock and Tony Corry for pages 1, 19, 20, 21a, 21b, 22, 23a, 23b, 24, 25, 28, 29, 30, 31, 32, 33, 34, 36, 37, 38, 39, 40a, 40b, 45, 46, 47a, 47b, 49, 52, 54, 55, 56a, 57, 58, 59, 61b, 63b, 64, 66, 67a, 66b, 71, 73b, 79, 80, 81, 89b, 90, 97a, 97b, 98, 114, 115, 119, 127, 130, 134, 135, 141, 143, 152, 153a, 153b, 155, 156, 159, 160, 161a, 162a, 162b, 164, 165, 168, 169, 170, 171, 172, 173, 174-5, 177, 178, 179, 181a, 181b, 182, 184, 185a, 191, 192, 193, 195a, 195b, 202, 210; To Tony Corry for 146-7; To Terence Reeves-Smyth for 78, 117a, 117b, 129b, 144, 145b, 185b; The Ian H. Clare Collection (EHS) 9; The Dean Collection (EHS) 86, 87, 91b; To the National Trust for 74, 75, 100, 101, 102-3, 108, 109, 112, 113, 120, 121, 131; Lambeth Palace Library 60, 61a, 62, 63a; The Earl of Erne 85a; Irish Architectural Archive 87b.